"...he fate of the Gael is to lose everything."

Cape Wrath

L. Inchard
L. Laxfor
Scourie
Quinag
L. Assynt
Suilven
L. Broom
Slioch
L. Rosque
L. Fannich

Rhiconick
L. Stack
L. More
A. Merkland
Lock Shin
Lairg

Kyle of Durness
Loch Eriboll
L. Hope
B. Hope
Kyle of Tongue
Tongue
Bettyhill
B. Loyal
Loyal
L. Naver
B. Clibreck

Thurso

Caithness Wick

Sutherland

Ross

The Moray Firth

Black Isle

Autumns in Skye:
Ross·
·and·
·Sutherland·

"Is beag an tigh anns an toll càirdean"
"A wee house holds friends"

T. Ratcliffe Barnett — 1930

AUTUMNS IN SKYE
ROSS & SUTHERLAND

EILAN DONAN CASTLE

AUTUMNS IN SKYE ROSS & SUTHERLAND

T. RATCLIFFE BARNETT

WITH 24 ILLUSTRATIONS FROM
PHOTOGRAPHS BY
DOUGLAS GUTHRIE
AND
ARCHIBALD E. ROBERTSON

JOHN GRANT BOOKSELLERS LTD.
EDINBURGH: 31 GEORGE IV BRIDGE
LONDON: 98 GREAT RUSSELL STREET, W.C.
1946

FIRST EDITION . . . 1930
NEW AND REVISED EDITION . 1946

PRINTED IN GREAT BRITAIN BY
OLIVER AND BOYD LTD., EDINBURGH

TO

ALL THOSE EXILED SCOTS

WHO HAVE WRITTEN TO ME
FROM THE FOUR QUARTERS OF
THE EARTH—WITH A LONGING
IN THEIR HEARTS FOR THE
PEAT REEK AND THE SOFT
SMIRR OF HIGHLAND RAIN ON
THEIR FACES—MAY THIS BOOK
BRING SOME ADDED HINT
OF HOME

ISLE OF MY HEART

SKYE OF THE COOLINS

TO THE MEMORY OF THAT GREAT SKYEMAN—SHERIFF NICOLSON

Down the long winding streets of romance
    Walk I enchanted,
Where all my heart-strings of love are twined
    Round each tall dwelling,
And the sea haar is kissed by the warm
    Sunlight from heaven.

Oft do I brood on the high rock shrine,
    Lost in old mem'ries ;
Seeing the clansmen stript for the fight
    With foreign foemen ;
Hearing the sennachies proudly sing
    Scotland's brave story.

But, when the west wind blows from the hills
    Over the lowlands,
And all the fields are braided with green,
    Firstfruits of harvest,
Then, O my heart, I hear the call
    Of the dear islands ;

And of that road which stretches far north
    Over the moorlands,
Where the blue mountains, like sentries, stand
    Guarding the green glens ;
Land of brave heroes long since sleeping
    After their battles.

There, buoyed above the restless sea waves,
    Brown sails all flapping,
Riding in sunlight the birlinn waits
    To take me over ;
Fresh breezes whispering songs of love
    Through rope and rattling.

Over to Skye, the Isle of my Heart,
    Where in the old years
When youth and glamour glowed on my brow
    I found great wonders.
Splintered mountains in splendour rising
    Into the heavens ;

Sea lochs crowded with Viking stories,
    And castles hoary ;
Green straths dotted with old black houses,
    Where dwelt fine seamen ;
Peat reek rising like evening incense
    From homely altars.

Round each grey castle Ossian's giants
    Had great encounters ;
Bragela, queen of the Misty Isle,
    And mighty Cuchullin ;
Epics of battle, idylls of love,
    Still told in ceilidh.

Gone are the chieftains, ruined their halls,
    Centuries old now ;
Stark walls on headlands washed by the rain
    Gleam in the sunbursts ;
Wind from the Coolins sighing laments
    Over the lost days.

Oft in my wakeful hours do I dream
    Of thy wild mountains
Rising like blue clouds out of the sea
    In summer sunshine ;
Hearing the lilt of soft Gaelic tongues
    Bidding me welcome.

Yours be the love, O Skye, that outlives
    All generations ;
Burning, like peat fires that never die,
    For thy dear people ;
Home of my Heart and Isle of my Dreams,
    Skye of the Coolins.

EDINBURGH, *May* 1930

FOREWORD

THOMAS DE QUINCEY—that celestial tramp—in his " Confessions of an English Opium-Eater," comments on the justness of a remark of Dr Johnson, that " we never do anything for the last time (of things, that is, which we have long been in the habit of doing) without sadness of heart."

Having now reached the farthest bounds of Scotland, I must confess to a certain feeling of regret that this is the last of a series of six travel books on the Lowlands and Highlands which have given me much pleasure to write. Several of the articles have appeared in *The Scotsman* ; one or two are reprinted from the *S.M.T. Magazine* ; and that on " The Ten Commandments of Walking " was given as a wireless talk. For permission to reprint them, I am indebted to the editors of these journals, and to the British Broadcasting Corporation.

In every book of travel there must of necessity be a large number of historic statements, and there is nothing easier than making a slip. But, having done my best to verify every statement, I now gladly acknowledge the countless authorities to which I am indebted, and also the various poets quoted, without whose golden words some of the chapters would have lost their richest touch.

So long as there are roads in this beloved land, each generation will set out anew to discover traveller's joy. To one and all who seek the unspeakable pleasures which I myself have tasted, I can only say—May Good Luck attend you.

T. R. B.

CONTENTS

SKYE

		PAGE
I. THE ROAD TO SKYE		I
FROM LAGGAN TO KYLE		
II. THE SPLASH NET		8
A DREAM OF THE WESTERN ISLES		
III. SKYE		14
THE ISLAND OF MY HEART		
IV. CORUISK		20
THE LOCH OF MYSTERY		
V. HEBRIDEAN MEMORIES		27
THE LURE OF THE ISLES		
VI. THE MAN OF SILENCE		33
A RAINBOW DAY IN THE FOREST		
VII. THE BORERAIG BAGPIPE		40
A PIPER'S PILGRIMAGE		
VIII. THE FINEST ROAD IN SKYE		48
FROM KYLE TO DUNVEGAN		
IX. SLEAT-OF-THE-WAVES		56
THE GARDEN OF SKYE		
X. CASTLES IN SKYE		64
DUNSCAITH : DUNTULM : DUNVEGAN		
XI. SCUIR NAN GILLEAN		76
THE PEAK OF THE YOUNG MEN		
XII. THE BRAVE SONS OF SKYE		81
AN INCOMPARABLE RECORD		
XIII. PABBAY		90
THE ISLAND OF THE PRIEST		

CONTENTS

ROSS

PAGE

XIV. THE SEA GATES OF WESTER ROSS . . . 96
I.—BRAEMORE, BROOM, AND DUNDONELL

XV. THE SEA GATES OF WESTER ROSS . . . 104
II.—GRUINARD, EWE, AND GAIRLOCH

XVI. A DREAM OF ISLE MAREE 112
SOUNDS OF THE SUMMER NIGHT

XVII. SUDDEN SUMMER 120
A SUNBURST AT GAIRLOCH

XVIII. GLEN TORRIDON 126
AND THE ROAD TO DIABAIG

XIX. THE OLD ROAD TO THE TIGH DIGE . . . 133
OR THE ART OF WALKING SLOW

XX. PREACHING CAVES 139
BY THE WESTERN SEA

XXI. THE FINDING OF RED RIVER 147
AN ADVENTURE IN FRIENDSHIP

SUTHERLAND

XXII. WANDERINGS IN SUTHERLAND 153
A CURE FOR WINTER WEARINESS

XXIII. THE WORSHIP STONES OF EDDRACHILLIS . . 161
A WILD TEMPLE

XXIV. HIGHLAND RAIN 166
ON LAND AND SEA

XXV. HAUNTS OF THE VIKINGS 172
ROUND THE SHORES OF SUTHERLAND

XXVI. THE ISLAND OF HANDA 180
A BIRD SANCTUARY

XXVII. THE UNSEEN HOST 186
AND THE HOUSE OF HOSPITALITY

XXVIII. THE TEN COMMANDMENTS OF WALKING . . 192
A TRAMPER'S DECALOGUE

LIST OF ILLUSTRATIONS
By DOUGLAS GUTHRIE

EILAN DONAN CASTLE . . . . *Frontispiece*

	PAGE
UIG BAY, ISLE OF SKYE	6
LOCH CORUISK	20
ROAD TO THE COOLINS, SKYE	52

By ARCHIBALD E. ROBERTSON

	PAGE
LOCHIEL'S COUNTRY, LOCH ARKAIG	5
IN GLEN AFFRIC	12
THE ISLAND OF EIGG	29
MACLEOD'S TOMB, RODIL CHURCH	30
HARRIS FROM BERNERA	32
THE COOLIN RIDGE FROM BRUACH NA FRITHE	49
LOCH CORUISK, SKYE	61
DUNVEGAN CASTLE	68
SLIGACHAN AND SGURR NAN GILLEAN	77
STRATH NA SHEALLAG, DUNDONNELL	100
THE KING'S HIGHWAY, GRUINARD	109
SLIOCH, LOCH MAREE	114
LIATHACH FROM GLEN TORRIDON	127
BEINN EIGHE FROM LOCH COULIN	144
A BLACK HOUSE	148
NORTH WEST SUTHERLAND	157
BEN LAOGHAL, TONGUE	163
BALNAKEILL CHURCH, DURNESS	174
LOCH STACK, SUTHERLAND	180
AN TEALLACH : TOLL AN LOCHAIN	189

SKYE

I

THE ROAD TO SKYE

FROM LAGGAN TO KYLE

My heart is yearning for thee, O Skye !
Dearest of islands !

IT was a hot September day when the sea hunger put
a spell on me. The Braes of Badenoch were like the
hills of heaven in the heat haze, but in Cluny's country
you are far from the sea. When the sea calls it turns
your heart like a lover's song. There is nothing for it,
then, but to shoulder your bundle, hitch up the tartan,
cock the blue bonnet, and go. So, whistling the tune
that all wandering fellows know, I turned my back on
Badenoch, and took the long road for Skye. Every step
westward was lighter than the last, and when I swung
down Glen Spean at four to the hour the river was
laughing, but not louder than my heart.

I passed the burial cairns, near Mulroy, which
mark the spot where one of the last clan battles was
fought—those nine rough memorials of stone, on the
tallest of which there is a cross and the name of a
Macdonald. I was now in the region of the new
electric power works, and could hear the workmen
driving the tunnel on the far side of the tumbling

Spean. Just then I spied a fellow-traveller approaching
with the gay steps of one who has been drowning his
sorrows. When he caught sight of the ribbons fluttering
on the breeze, his heart overflowed, and he straightway
embraced me as a friend. Then, standing on the
sunny road, I got all his story, and we were quite
oblivious to the passers-by. He had been to Confession,
and was just new come from a Mass, and from something newer forby. He was eloquent of the good he had
got from the dear old priest, who himself had baptised
in his long curacy of souls seven baby boys who have
since that become priests. I was in no mood to argue,
so I seconded every sentiment of the gay lad, who
parted from me with the most affectionate of farewells,
naming a howf in Glasgow where we might meet
again. By all that is good in the weakest human
creature, who would not love such a jolly penitent on
a day of sun and beauty ?

Then, on again, with a look at the old chapel of
St Margaret's at Mulroy, and the way soon led past
Kilmonivaig, with a swing northwards to Invergloy and
the Great Glen.

To tell the story of the Great Glen would be to tell
the tale of a dozen clans. Striking westward from the
Great North Road, which now runs up the west side
of Loch Lochy, Loch Oich, and Loch Ness, are four
of the most romantic outgaits to the sea in the Highlands.

The first begins at Lochiel's domain of Achnacarry
and leads along Loch Arkaig, by Glen Pean and Glen
Dessary, to those most beautiful of western lochs—
blessed Morar, the deepest bit of fresh water in Scotland ; and heavenly Nevis of the sea-wrack, which
worms its way between great mountains to the very
heart of Tearlach Og's own land. At every milestone

a man with an ear for romantics can hear the march of the Cameron men.

The next outgait to the west is Glen Garry, with its bluff old castle guarding the very door of the Macdonald territory, and many another secret that lies behind it concerning that gallant, Pickle the Spy.

Still farther north comes Glen Moriston, the long glen of the Grants, which runs right to Loch Duich, with its fine story of the eight Glen Moriston men who hid the Prince in a cave at Coiraghoth for three days in June 1746.

What tales might not one tell at a *ceilidh* round the peats of those four outgaits to the Western Seas ! But the road to Skye is far too long for any man to taigle over such historic gallantries.

I spent a night on a shakedown at Old Kilcumin, where the monks' bells keep you so cheery all through the night that there is with me, at least, never any chance of sleeping in. So I rose in the dark and took the road down to the loch side, and I can smell the sweet scents of morning yet as I passed through the village in the ghostly half-lights. A wondrous dawn was putting out the stars, and the early morning winds blew fresh and caller about the knees. Memories arose of a trek made long years ago up the other side of the loch to Inverness by Foyers and Inverfarigaig. But to-day I am to find a new story about older days than these, at a little house three miles beyond Invermoriston —Altsaigh—near by a stream that comes tumbling down a ravine from the slopes of Mealfourvounie. Here is a tale of clan feuds that is surely hard to beat for butchery !

It all began at Kilchrist, or Cille-Chriosda, a little place on the green flats near Beauly, and the quarrel

was between the MacKenzies of Kintail and the Glengarry Macdonalds. Many of the bloodiest deeds of
warfare seem to have been done on the Lord's own
Day—for it was a Sunday when Glengarry's men
found the chapel of Cille-Chriosda full of MacKenzie
men, women, and children. In those sad old days of
Highland feuds there was always some older score to
wipe out. The MacKenzies had slain the sons of the
Macdonalds at some time or other before this. So
here was the enemy delivered into the Macdonalds'
hands. The word was sent round. The thatched
chapel was set on fire. Those who rushed for the
door were met by a claymore death. Glengarry's piper,
fey with inspiration, marched round the blazing church
playing a sudden piobaireachd which has ever since
been known as *Cille Chriosda*, or Glengarry's March.
Thus the shrieks of the dying were silenced by the
screaming pipes. A terrific tune and no mistake.

Then, here at Altsaigh, came the sequel. For the
MacKenzies were soon on the red road that leads to
revenge. They overtook a party of Glengarry's men
resting near this very burn of Altsaigh. The claymore
flashed, the clan cries rose, and the fight began. But
the Macdonalds were outnumbered, so they fled towards
the burn. They missed the ford, were caught on the
edge of the ravine, and there the MacKenzies either
slew them or sent them to certain death in the abyss
below. But one gallant lad, called Alan MacRaonuill,
made for a place where the stream rushes through a
yawning chasm. It was a desperate leap ; but life lay
on the other side, and death was at his heels. The
Macdonald giant took the jump, and reached the
other side. The MacKenzie, a smaller man, but with
a fire of hate in his heart, leaped after him. He just

LOCHIEL'S COUNTRY, LOCH ARKAIG

missed the further bank, slithered down it, and caught hold of a birch tree. There he hung suspended over the death cauldron. Then Alan MacRaonuill turned back, leaned over, saw his enemy hanging on the tree. With his eyes looking straight into the eyes of his foe, he hissed out these words—" I have left too much behind me with you this day, so take this also." And with that he cut off the birch branch with his dirk. Then Alan ran to the loch, plunged in, and before he had time to swim across a boat put out from the other side and picked him up.

But it is a far cry to Skye. After Inverness it is a long road round by Dingwall, Strathbraan, and Strathcarron to the sea. After Garve the road passes through an unbroken series of deer forests—Strathgarve, Coirriemoillie, Lochluichart, Ledgowan, Achnashellach, Attadale, and many more to the north and south. A fine wild world when the sun shines. But the rain set in, and not for the first time did I seek shelter in the Skye Railway, which is the most cautious concern in Scotland. Nearly thirty years ago I travelled on this railway. The guard had just got a new uniform, so it meant a long gossip at every station while the tale was told and he showed off his braid and buttons. That night we arrived an hour late at Strome Ferry. For the nearer you get to Skye the more time there is to spare.

In mist and rain Loch Carron loomed inhospitable. Yonder, across the grey water, was Jeantown. But at least here was the red wrack on the shore, and the rain tasted salt even at Attadale.

What is it that draws the heart of an islander when he gets within sight of the sea ? In France a wounded Highlander once exclaimed to me when he reached the convoy platform at Etretat in the gloom—" I smell the

sea ! " It is an old ageless hunger which was put
there by his forbears, whose lives were spent on the
tumbling waters, the spindrift in their hair, the brown
tan of sunshine and storm on their cheeks, and the
laughter of the seas in the clear blue of their far-away
eyes. Here are the old primeval songs of the sea as it
breaks on the grey rocks, tangles of brown wrack
rising and falling on the tide, sea birds screaming,
and the old boat glucking on the waves by the slippery
pier.

Across the strait—Skye ! The island that has a
story to tell the heart of those who love her which no
other Hebrid isle can tell. An isle of ethereal beauties
when the sun shines out of the summer sky and the
Coolins pierce the cloudless blue in the distance like
the fairy peaks of heaven. But an isle of tragic secrets
when the rain drives in sheets and the mist creeps down
the deathly rocks like a thief by Scavaig and eerie
Coruisk, with only the sound of the mad stream
whispering a coronach in the black night. An island
of brave sons, old-world legendry, terrific mountains,
and sunny green glens running down to the sea, where
in peaceful silence old men tend their little crofts and
cailleachs throw another peat on the everlasting fires.

After all those years, Skye again ! These white
cottages ; this verdant machar by the shore ; the racing
tides, the distant islands—Raasay, Scalpay, Pabbay,
Longay, and the Crowlins—appearing and vanishing
in sunshine and shower as the clouds lift or settle ;
white-winged boats beating through the narrows, which
call up dreams of Haco and his Vikings, who gave the
very name to the place ; and the Norse princess who
sat in Caisteal Maol and took toll of every ship. The
wind blows fresh and salt from the sea. The birds

UIG BAY, ISLE OF SKYE

are wailing on the edge of the tide. The rain is over, and the great clouds are banked in wild glory as the sun goes down. The red hills loom against the evening sky. The sea hunger is satisfied. I am come home once more, for the salt spray is on my face.

Late that night I took the road by the sea to say good-night to Skye. Great waves were breaking, and the west wind blew from the hills. In front, a dark tree-clad promontory, inky black against the sky, which held in it only one star, with a hint of the rising moon behind the clouds. In the pitchy shadow of the trees by the shore, a strange glow of light, which grew larger and more diffuse the nearer I drew. It was a little round gipsy tent, with a fire glowing at the door. A woman was sitting in the red arch of light—warm, happy, speaking low—like a Madonna in a halo of glory. Then the moon rode out, and the glowing fire was swallowed up in the white radiance which put out all lesser lights.

Peace be to thee and thy children, O Skye !
Dearest of islands !

II

THE SPLASH NET

A DREAM OF THE WESTERN ISLES

To all appearance one fishing net is very much like another. And yet there are nets and nets, and a name makes all the difference. Call a herring net a splash net, and the local Sheriff may have something to say to you. So I shall relate a dream which I had long ago, for no man has ever been convicted on the evidence of a thirty-year-old dream.

It was in the middle 'nineties. We had thrashed our way through the Kyles of Bute to Blackfarland Bay. It was there one morning that, forgetful of the strength of the tide, I got up early, and, when no one was about, took a header from the deck. But I found when I appeared again that the yacht was a longer way off than she should have been. It was a hard swim to reach the dinghy again. When we rounded Ardlamont we caught the full force of half a gale in Loch Fyne, and had to pound along under shortened sail in drenching rain for Ardrishaig. Then, on a sunny morning, we were towed through the Crinan to the magic West, and raced northward through the tides of the Dorus Mhor to Oban, on the bluest of summer days, with a topsail breeze all the way.

Some old photographs lie before me. One of Oban Bay in the good old days when there was always a crowd of yachts, great and small, lying at their

moorings. It took some seamanship in those days to
steer the schooner between them to an anchorage
where she could ride out a storm and swing clear of
her neighbours in safety on a long chain. Another
shows the yacht lying in Tobermory Bay, with her
tall, rakish masts, and an innocent-looking brown net
drying on the davits. A third photograph, of the deck
when we were running down past Fladda, Lunga, and
the Dutchman's Cap, on the west of Mull—Malcolm,
the deck-hand, in his blue jersey, sitting on the bul-
warks, and Captain Mac, sitting in his brass buttons
on the hatchway by the foremast, mending the brown
net between them. That was indeed a glorious summer
day, and the old schooner, with every wing spread,
skimmed gracefully over the sapphire seas. It is not
wise, however, to hang out a splash net to dry on the
davits when there is a Post Office window in view, and
where the address of the next place of call is given to
the local postmaster for the forwarding of letters. But
the postmasters of both places must have retired from
service, if not from this life, long ago, and when we
anchored opposite the village which means the Foot of
the Little Waterfall, we made certain that not even the
seals that were basking on the rocks in the early morning
sun saw the net hanging on the davits. It was, however,
about that net I dreamed the following dream.

.   .   .   .   .   .

It had been a day of great heat in the Sound. For
hours we lay in the doldrums, becalmed " like a painted
ship upon a painted ocean," the great sails hanging
limp and useless. The white decks reflected the glare
of the sun, and the brasswork burned like fire. We were
off the coast of Mull—somewhere—and this blazing
day had been succeeded by one of those lambent

twilights which make the islands of the West almost
holy with a tranquil, other-world beauty. At last, when
the rose of sunset had faded from the sky and the stars
began to appear above the masts, we were compelled
to get into the dinghy and tow the schooner into a
lonely bay.   .

No house was near, but the sound of a stream filled
the night with husheen as the Western world fell
asleep. Captain Mac was a silent man and a good
skipper, with an intimate knowledge of every tide and
anchorage in the West. He seemed determined now
to anchor in this solitary bay. So the anchor went out
at last with a rattle and a roar, the sails were housed,
the gaskets were securely tied round the boom, and after
the long day we all went below, and were soon fast
asleep.

Sometime in the small hours I heard the sound of
stealthy footsteps on deck, the whispered converse of
two men speaking in Gaelic, and the boat being brought
alongside. In my dream I seemed to have lain down
in my bunk without undressing, having tucked my
pyjamas under my head for a pillow. Slipping out of
the cabin and up the companionway, I arrived on deck
just in time to hear a quiet voice from the boat saying,
" Jump in."

With that I was sitting in the stern sheets, while
the boat was being silently rowed to the shore. It was
very dark for a summer night, but I saw, or rather felt
the net heaped up in the bottom of the boat, and I
noticed that a thin crescent moon was hanging in the
sky like a silver sickle above the loom of the hills.

When we reached the burnside Captain Mac got
out, took hold of one end of the net, and told Malcolm
to pay out slowly, while I rowed the boat across the burn

mouth to the shingle on the other side. Here Malcolm, still holding his end, got out, and the long net sagged in a great semicircle across the burn mouth.

Not a sound of an oar in the water, not a word spoken, each man standing by, quietly waiting, while the third sat in the boat, which was grounded by the burnside, all listening to the sound of falling water in the summer night. The world of men and cities seemed very far away, and the beauty of the balmy night was wonderful.

I was just beginning to calculate how long the silence had lasted, when there was a sound of splashing on the other side of the burn. Malcolm bestirred himself, and he too began splashing the water. Each man splashed and drew in, splashed and drew in regularly, until the sweep of the horse-shoe net grew less and less across the mouth of the stream. Any fish that were not already caught, and might be heading for the sea when the splashing began, were now secure in the net. The splash and draw-in was heavy work, and each man was thoroughly soaked as he stood in the water and worked monotonously.

" Are you sure there is no one about ? " I whispered.

" Ach, no, sir ; Tobermory is a long way off, and big John Campbell, the polis at the village down the Sound, is away at his cousin's wedding."

Meantime, Malcolm had been slowly coiling his end of the net into the boat as the splashing went on. He now stopped, launched the boat, got in, and with a stroke or two of the oars brought the boat up and across the stream, landing beside Captain Mac. The net was now a bag from which nothing could escape.

Then the real excitement began. The whispered Gaelic went on as the net came in. Was it heavy or light ? In my dream I seemed to see a glitter of silver again and again, and many other things. Splash and silver. The thin sickle of the moon. Salt water dripping. The smell of seawrack. The sound of the stream. The quiet dip of oars. The black loom of the yacht. The tall masts pointing to the stars that hung in the velvet sky—and the stars themselves were winking, winking curiously as if they saw some humour in the mad world down-by. Then the dreamer slid into a sound sleep and knew no more.

Next morning the tinkle of a bell awoke us. The sun was streaming through the skylight and blazing hot on the decks, which had all been swabbed clean and white. Malcolm was burnishing the brass on the binnacle. Captain Mac was walking slowly up and down, looking at the weather and the ropes.

" A fine morning for a swim, but the water will be cold," said he.

" A fine morning, indeed," I replied, " but I had a strange dream last night ! "

" Well, well, but the cold water will soon put the dreams out of you."

Just then I heard the sound of frying fish in the fo'c'sle. With a laugh, I raised my hands and took a clean header into the strong salt sea—so green and iridescent below, so full of rushing music in the ears, so buoyant to swim in when the sunlit surface was reached. Then a scramble up the gangway that had been let down, with a white fender on either side— another header and another swim—two or three strong men in the water side by side. Sunlight, morning winds, glowing health, joy of living, care-free souls, and nothing on the horizon but hope !

Then, with appetites as keen as a razor's edge, we

IN GLEN AFFRIC

sat down at the snowy table in the saloon, and Henry the steward brought in a dish of the most delicious sea trout !

" I dreamed last night . . . ! " I began again.

" Never mind what you dreamed—tuck in," said another.

And the sea trout were as fresh as if they had come straight from a burn-mouth but an hour ago.

> Sing me a song of a lad that is gone,
>   Say, could that lad be I ?
> Merry of soul he sailed on a day
>   Over the sea to Skye.
>
> Mull was astern, Rum on the port,
>   Eigg on the starboard bow ;
> Glory of youth glowed in his soul :
>   Where is that glory now ?
>
> Give me again all that was there,
>   Give me the sun that shone !
> Give me the eyes, give me the soul,
>   Give me the lad that's gone !
>   ROBERT LOUIS STEVENSON.

III

SKYE

THE ISLAND OF MY HEART

I NEVER think of the Isle of Skye but I am reminded of three great English writers who, one after the other, determined to write an adequate appreciation of that superb Hebrew drama—the Book of Job. The wonder of it so oppressed them that they never could make a beginning. So they all died without having put pen to paper.

And yet! the Isle of Mist is so compelling that the veriest scribbler keeps writing love notes on it every time he thinks of the heavenly days and magic nights he has spent in that paradise of the West.

In winter time, when the fog rolls along the city streets, and all the beauties of the world are blotted out in gloom, the Skye-lover will plough his way through the crowd with a far-ben look on his face and lips that keep muttering some soundless rune. At that moment he is seeing the distant Coolins, blue and ethereal. The summer sun is blazing down on the purple heather at his feet, and the warm air is drugged with the scent of honey and bog-myrtle. Instead of the roar of city traffic he hears the crash of great seas on the mighty headlands of Bracadale, or the wind roaring in the shrouds of the old boat as she thrashes her way between Hunish Head and Trodday Isle, her dripping bows pointing bravely across the Minch for the Outer Isles.

It was this undying hunger in the heart that made Alexander Nicolson write—

> My heart is yearning for thee, O Skye,
> Dearest of islands.

It is this same compulsion of love that makes it as inevitable for the wandering man to unburden himself about Skye, as for the lover to be for ever sending passionate epistles to the mistress of his heart.

Skye! The Isle of Mist. The Winged Isle. Eilean a Cheo. Eilean Sgitheanach—the Island of Skyants or Skye Folks. Call it what you will, the very name has something mystical about it, something of that high geste which fills the soul with dreams of Ossian's heroes, and brings you very near the island rovers who lived of old in yon stark castles which turn their eyeless windows to the grumbling seas.

There are many ways of approaching Skye. You may travel all the way from London to Kyle in a touring car, and cross the narrow strait in an open ferry-boat, your luxurious glass coach perched precariously on two planks placed athwart the gunwales. Then, when you scramble out on the stone pier at Kyleakin, you will be standing on the very doorstep of Skye. But, although that is a glamorous road to Skye, yet it is not the best.

I like to remember that I saw Skye first from the white deck of a schooner as we raced northwards from Mull on a blue day in June. Those were the days long before auxiliary screws or motor-cars. From a bundle of old faded notebooks I have found the very year. But that is my own story. From Tobermory

Bay, round Ardnamurchan, and up the Sound of Sleat
we sailed, all though the livelong day, until in the
evening we dropped anchor at Isle Ornsay.

What a run north that was! With a top-sail
breeze, and every sail drawing to perfection, so long
as the man at the tiller kept his eye on the leech.
Moidart, Arisaig, Morar of the white sands, and
Knoydart of the lonely sea lochs—Prince Charlie's
own land—on the starboard side; with Eigg, Rhum,
and the green lands of Sleat on the port. The soft
summer wind sang in the shrouds, and the blue seas
sweeshed along the lee gunwale in white foam. Climbing the rattlings, I sat on the cross-trees, one arm
round the mast, swinging with the plunging ship in
perfect happiness, far above the little black people
on the deck. The seabirds circled and screamed
above the fluttering burgee at the masthead, and I
was all alone with my dreams betwixt the sea and
the sky.

Yonder was Skye! The dim Coolins rising in
serrated loveliness against the blue-white heavens. A
whole world of Celtic legendry, romance, and history
hidden behind these mighty mountains, and up these
sea lochs, and along these shores, which, as yet, I had
never visited. Looking back to-day, after many years,
during which I have travelled almost every road in
Skye, viewed the Hebridean world from a pinnacle of
the Coolins, explored the sea lochs, and been drawn
back again and again by this island of my heart, I envy
the care-free lad who sat on the cross-trees singing to
himself as the white-winged yacht raced like a fair
adventuress for the island that had never been
visited!

This drawing power of Skye for a lover of beauty

and old romance must seem almost ludicrous to a
practical man who balances his weekly expenses to a
penny every Saturday night.

Well do I recall a visit to the town of Wick the very
year after my first view of Skye from the cross-trees.
I was clad in the sober garments which ten days'
residence in that Caithness metropolis required of a
Scottish probationer. But, tucked away in a needlessly
big bag were some old clothes and an older bonnet.
So, when twelve o'clock struck on the Sunday night I
ruined all my chances of a " call " back by taking the
midnight train—half-luggage and half-passenger—down
to Dingwall.

" We'll maybe see you back again," said the old
elder who carried my bag.

" Aye," added another, as he shook hands, " and
we'll maybe no' ! "

It was a dooms dreich night journey. The autumn
frosts had come, and I tumbled out at Dingwall,
shivering in the old clothes, as the grey dawn spread
over the sky. The Skye train was even slower than
the Highland had been. I was really making for
Glasgow ! But I was taking the longest possible way
in order to get another sniff of Skye. At that time the
railway terminus was at Strome Ferry. You scrambled
for a meal among a lot of Skye drovers in the Strome
Ferry Hotel, and then boarded the Portree boat down
at the pier. It was a dismal drizzle of mist and rain
all the way. At Portree the real Skye rain gave us a
drenching welcome as we walked up the pier. Mountainous seas kept us lively all the way to the Clyde, and
when we were rounding the Mull of Kintyre, the salt
spray was lashing over the funnel. But it was worth
it all. To those for whom the sea has no terrors the

salt wind and the crash of great waves make the
life-blood dance with joy. And I had seen Skye
again !

The Coolins—these mighty mountains, which from
the distance look like the fairy ramparts of heaven—will
to the end of the hundred thousand years preserve their
desolation from all languid motorists and slipper-footed
tourists. Their splintered peaks and far-off corries,
their deathly precipices and narrow rock ridges will
remain what they have always been—the sanctuary of
the strong and the climbers' paradise of peace.

To-day you will find solitude at Trumpan when
you dream of Lady Grange and the Battle of the Dykes.
Hot silence awaits you among the birch trees and
hazels as you wander down the road past Tokavaig to
Castle Dunscaith, the home of Sgathach the Warrior
Queen, and Cuchullin himself. If the soul of Alexander
Smith haunts the old House of Ord with its little
pointed windows on Loch Eishort, or the ghost of
Sheriff Nicolson revisits Husabost on its way to hear
the great Macrimmon play his phantom pipes at
Boreraig, the ancient silences will lend them aid to
their wanderings. The great seas still thunder about
the Neist and Dunvegan Head when the winter gales
roar across the Little Minch, and on the quiet summer
days there is a heavenly outgate from Bracadale or
Snizort to the misty islands that lie asleep on the
bosom of the tranquil sea.

The very thought of Skye mingles with my dreams.
For, on those rare occasions when I lie awake, I turn
my mind to the Misty Isle, and, beginning at Kyleakin,
I travel in fancy over every road in Skye, naming each
sea loch and township and clachan as I pass them in
my spiritual pilgrimage. A wandering man might well

lie awake o' nights for the sheer pleasure of such a
fairy jaunt. But by the time I have travelled by far
Duntulm or the lonely Point of Sleat, and am footing it
wearily past Lusa Bridge for home, the tides of Kyle
are racing through the drowsy world of forgetting,
where memory is no more, and I am sound asleep.

IV

CORUISK

THE LOCH OF MYSTERY

THIS weird loch, lying in a cup of the Coolins, miles
remote from the nearest house or travelling road, with
a sudden outfall to the sea-waves of Scavaig, is surely
the wildest bit of scenery in Scotland.

Not to know Coruisk is not to know Skye.

But how futile it is for anyone to sit down at a
table in the far-off city and catalogue the recorded
wonders of this savage spot by gathering facts from all
the well-known books on Skye, from the diaries of
dead travellers, or from the romantic poetry of Sir
Walter ! No true lover ever described the face of his
beloved in the language of another man. As with faces,
so with scenery. We must paint direct, always using
our own colours and brushes, the hand obeying the
understanding heart which looks out on this wonderful
world through a pair of undimmed eyes.

An old photograph lies before me. A group of men
standing on the shores of Coruisk in the middle 'nineties.
The great adventure had just begun for us all. The
lad with the plaid died as the Mayor of a South African
town. The tall, dark man with the yachting cap went
down with the *Lusitania* when she was torpedoed in
the Atlantic. The name of the third man is known in
every corner of the world to-day, wherever collectors

20

LOCH CORUISK

pick up the finest of etchings. The fourth man, with the blue bonnet, is still exploring the by-ways of Scotland and the highways of the heart. The unseen man who worked the cumbersome, old-fashioned camera has stood before kings, yet has never lost the common touch. Thus, even the loneliest spots on earth are haunted with the ghosts of the past.

It was a June day. We had sailed across to Skye from Loch Scresort, in the Island of Rhum. The laughing summer seas, the sunny deck, the great banks of snow-white clouds floating lazily in the blue, the favouring breeze which made the voyage a sailor's luxury, with the white birds flashing above us and screaming as with delight—it is all as if it had happened yesterday.

Then the mighty Coolins, which always seem so fairy-like from a distance, began to close down upon us with a frown of anger as we entered Loch Scavaig. Slowly we came to anchor, far up in the narrow neck of the loch, where the tiny islands are. A warp was fixed to an iron ring on the rock to starboard, and another to the ring on the rock to port. Then the great seabird folded her white wings, and was at rest for the night.

Standing on the deck, we felt very small in that wild place. Garsven towered above us in all its rocky splendour. The Mad Stream fell down the cliff with a constant hush of mystery. The wind had fallen. In the silence our voices sounded loud and aggressive, as if we were intruding in some other-world preserve of lost souls. Scrambling over the narrow bastion of rocks which separate the fresh water of Coruisk from the salt water of Scavaig, we soon came to the great boulder which is known to all wanderers round these shores. There, before us, lay the loch—silent, eerie, grim.

The grassless mountains rose on every side, encircling the cauldron of water. There was no sign of life anywhere. No birds on the naked hills. No red deer on the slopes of Druim-na-ramh. As the long summer day declined the gloom settled on Coruisk—a blue dusk which gradually deepened into an inky night, making the details invisible. And yet this ghostly gloom of the Coolins was exaggerated by the fact that behind that terrific rampart of rocks the afterglow of sunset was still shining, and so the long serrated ridge quivered with sensibility where the inky hills met the luminous sky.

That night it seemed as if we were living in the deeps of another world. A star or two came out in the velvet firmament above the tall masts. There was something unearthly in the thought of falling asleep in this abysmal cauldron of Scavaig to the never-ending husheen of the Mad Stream. Night at Coruisk is a very different thing from day. The awful gloom and silence suggest death.

Suddenly there was a quiver of light to the north above the black hills. Then another, and another, until the whole sky was illumined with the fires of the Northern Lights. It was the last touch needed to give the sense of the unutterable to the midnight scene, as flash after flash came from the soundless guns of heaven.

But the next morning we awoke to stern reality. A southerly wind was blowing right into the loch. We had taken our risk, and were now caught in the neck of the narrows. How easy to-day for a sailing boat with an auxiliary motor to face any head wind. But, in the old days, it was all a matter of sails and seamanship against wind and tide. The problem was, how to hoist sail, weigh anchor, and get enough way on to beat out of the narrows on very short tacks, without drifting on the sunken rocks. All hands were at their stations.

The anchor was hove short. The bow fell away to catch the wind, but had to be brought up again for the other tack almost before there was any speed on the little ship. It was " 'Bout ship " again and again. Then the inevitable happened. The sea lifted her fore-foot, and she began to plunge. At the next plunge she bumped keel on. We had hit a sunken rock. She quivered from stem to stern like a living thing outraged.

Captain Mac rapped out an appropriate sailor word. Every man did what he was told. But the sea-cook— who knew nothing of the way of ships—stood holding on to a rope, as white as one of his own soda scones, with teeth chattering, in a sheer funk. More than one eye calculated the distance it would be to swim ashore at the Bad Step. But at the next plunge, which we all feared, she was in deep water. She gathered way, and laying over to the breeze, she was safe. Within an hour we were racing close-hauled for the Point of Sleat. Such was my first coming to Coruisk.

Years passed, and two men pitched their camp on the shores of that uncanny loch. They were both artists. For what painter has not longed to make an immortal picture of Coruisk ? Could anyone find a more isolated spot for a dwelling-place ? The Isle of Soay is three miles off by water. To the nearest house at Camusunary it is a good three miles' walk round a desolate shore. Sligachan is eight miles distant across Druimhain, and the track lies down one of the wildest glens in Scotland. I have said that at night the gloom of Coruisk suggests death. It was more than that to the two painters. Death actually came, stalking down the cauldron side like a black shadow. One of them died, and the other was left alone with the body of his friend to people the solitude. Ever since, even on the brightest summer day, Coruisk has been a sinister place to me.

My last visit to Coruisk was but a year or two ago. The day was one of God's poems—all blue and white and sunny. When the rest of the world was deluged with floods of rain, Skye smiled serene in the sunlight. That is Skye. Celestial beyond our dreams when all the world weeps, and wetter than the worst place when the fat Southern shires are sweltering in the sun.

We took the road to Elgol by Broadford and Kil-Christ. Mighty Blaven rose above the green shores of Loch Slapin in all the glory of cliff and corrie and scree. The road hugs the shore round the head of the loch, and from Faolean you look across to fine sheeplands and the long, low nose of Rhu Suisnish ending in a little cliff. Up and up the rough road climbs, over the green moors, and round the shoulders of little Ben Meabost. And from Elgol post office, Eigg, Rhum, and Canna are lying out on the summer seas before you.

The road plunges down a steep hill to the shore. Here the boat lay waiting by the inhospitable beach, with Sandy, Angus, and Donald aboard. In the most out-of-the-way places in Skye you will see men wearing old blue jerseys, which they brought home many years ago after a season of the Clyde yachting. To-day the name of more than one famous yacht adorns the breasts of the Skye boatmen. So it was at Elgol.

The boat had a motor engine, but there is not always comfort in that thought. The engine would not start. After much palaver, we hoisted the ancient brown sail, while Angus and Donald coaxed the engine and kept giving it an unwise number of drinks.

" She will be all right in a minute ; she is only a wee bit ill-natured," was the continual refrain.

Another spate of Gaelic and English about paraffin oil, sparking plugs, and choked pipes.

"She will be all right. We came over from Soay this morning."

Doubtless.

So we held on under sail. But it was slow work.

At last, by one of those lucky chances which even a skilled engineer could scarce explain, the engine got over its ill-temper and became good-natured. That is the delightsome thing about the isles. In spite of everything, you always get there, somehow and sometime.

That day the gloom of Coruisk was wondrously illumined. The Coolins were sleeping in beauty, without a suggestion of storm or tragedy or death. The outgait to Rhum and Eigg was a perfect dream of pearl and blue. Old days or new, sad memories or gay, here was the indescribable mystery, the solemn grandeur, and a peace that was almost holy.

But the wind was freshening, and the blue sea was now foam-flecked. Angus brought over the boat from the little island to the rocks beside the sandy bay. It was significant that Angus and Donald were still tinkering with the moody engine.

We set out bravely at last, with the motor chugging unevenly, like a long leg and a short. To steady the now plunging boat we determined to hoist the sail. When the old patched canvas was nearly set, I laid my heavy hands on the halliard and hoisted the sail home. The rotten rope broke. Down came the sail and the great spar with a rattle, smothered us all, and hit some on the head. A spate of Gaelic was met by a torrent of English. The boat crashed on through the rising seas under the power of the lame motor. But, despite ill-natured engines and rotten ropes, we got there.

My memories of Elgol that day circle round a splendid tea, a spotless kitchen, and a curious picture of the poet Burns. There is also a vision of a sweet old Highland lady in a pure white mutch, who had no English, and had never been out of Elgol in her long life of eighty-four years. The oleograph portrait of Burns was doubtless a German print. The face was quite recognisable, but the dress was grotesque. He had a plaid over his shoulder, lace ruffles hanging about his wrists, and the delicate, lady-like fingers of a dilettante who had never done a day's work or held a plough.

But these are mere incidentals, like the lame motor and the rotten halliard.

The mystery of Coruisk, like the beauty of old age and the grace of human kindness, remains.

> Blessings be on ye, both now and aye,
>   Dear human creatures !
> Yours is the love that no gold can buy,
>   Nor time can wither.
> Peace be to thee, and thy children, O Skye !
>   Dearest of Islands.

V

HEBRIDEAN MEMORIES

THE LURE OF THE ISLES

THERE is a strange yearning in the soul of some of us to be always stepping farther westwards towards the lands of the setting sun. I never look out from the shores of Wester Ross but I wish to be on Skye ; and I never stand on a mountain-top or headland of Skye but I long to be setting out again for the Hebrides. Nor was I content till I had sailed sixty miles west of these outer isles and set my foot on that lonely rock in the Atlantic —St Kilda. It is the old argument to every wandering man, that when the sun goes down for the last time there must be some land of eternal bliss beyond all the islands and seas of this world.

So once more we stepped on board the old boat and set out from Skye for the Hebrides.

The morning was full of rain. But the glass was rising, and by the time we reached the Crowlins it was clear and dry. Thereafter it was one of God's own days all the way across the Minch to Harris—brilliant sun, blue seas, fine visibility, with pearly views of Skye and the Outer Isles.

We took the outside of Trodday, with the white light on the top, and its two red supply tanks on the cliff below, and set the course for Scalpay. Scalpay is a large green island at the mouth of Loch Tarbet, in Harris, with a population of about 700 souls. I have witnessed many homecomings to Scalpay, for the people there have kind hearts.

I have seen the salmon fishers from the Don and Dee and Tay returning when the fishing season was over—tall, upstanding lads, crowded together in the forecastle, full of merriment and Gaelic joviality. The men all joined hands, and, with the utmost solemnity, kept singing Hebridean croons and songs, swaying their hands and arms to keep the time. When the singing was over, the dancing began, to the music of a melodeon, with reels and steps and hoochs on the plunging boat. They never once lost their feet, nor did the solemnity ever leave their faces. Who shall blame them if they were seriously happy, for they were returning from that mainland world which seldom understands them, to their island home, which is all in all to them.

That day the bell on the Skeirigoe lightship, off Scalpay, sounded eerie on the tumbling waves, and squalls of stinging rain drove across the racing seas, to be followed again and again by sunbursts, which made the desolate hills of Harris look beautiful through the mist.

When we drew near Scalpay, little groups of men and women—mostly women—were standing on the hills and at the crofts, waving a welcome to the salmon fishers. At the pier a great crowd of excited women, with a few old men and boys, stood waiting. When at last the gangway was down and the salmon-fishers, in their good clothes and Sunday hats, stepped ashore, there was great hand-shaking and kissing. Every man returning seemed to kiss every girl and old woman present without exception, and no one seemed abashed. The women joked and smiled, and there was great

THE ISLAND OF EIGG

Gaelic, but still the lads never lost their gravity. Then, in twos and threes, they all went off to their own island crofts.

But to-day we were to witness a very different welcome. A great lady and her friends were on board, returning to a castle in Harris. For eleven years they had been exiles, as the estate had been bought by an industrial millionaire. Now, after his death, the estate had been bought back, and the old proprietor was returning. As we approached Scalpay we noticed a string of flags on the lighthouse, and through the glasses we read the one word " Welcome." At every house and croft on Harris or Scalpay home-made flags were flying and handkerchiefs were waving. An old *cailleach* stood on the shore and waved a white clout in each hand. At Scalpay pier the crowd clapped their hands and cheered. The boats were all beflagged. The lady stood on deck, dressed in a felt hat and a tweed coat closely buttoned up to the neck, and waved a smiling " Thank you " back. But, to the primitive mind, great folks are always supposed to be dressed in gorgeous raiment, and the beloved proprietrix did not understand a loud remark in Gaelic from a woman on the pier-head : " Oh, but isn't she awful plain ! "

When we left the pier the sun was shining brightly on the little run-rigs of corn which creep like green caterpillars among the rocks of the barren Harris shores. I never sail up Loch Tarbet but I gaze at these pathetic pockets of corn among the bogs, and at a roofless grey stone cottage. It was the home of a Harris man who spent his life as a shepherd on one of the Falkland Islands, near the Horn ; yet he came back to the old Hebridean home, built this house, and died happy on his own side of the world.

At Tarbet the pier was packed. A piper was playing. The lady, who was also returning to her island home, stepped ashore. Two pipers played " The Mackenzies' March " as she followed them to the pier-head. We all went ashore and heard the doctor's wife make a speech of welcome, to which the lady replied, that they had been very sad to leave eleven years ago, but were glad to return, and proud to be able to speak of " our tenants " once more ; for the laird is one who deals gently with the poorest crofter, and mixes a great deal of human kindness with his finance. Would that all our great Highland estates were owned to-day by men who know, and understand, and live among the people of the glens and islands !

At Rodel we saw the ancient church with its square tower—the cathedral of the Outer Isles—where you can look upon the original burial-place and monument of the Macleods. It is a place of mighty rocks, with a little harbour hidden behind them, and as you look at the old church, the barren rocks, and the heaving seas, a sense of old centuries rises up within you. Little wonder that they have called an old tune, " The Rocks of Rodel."

As we sailed south, the whole Hebridean world was shining in beauty. The isles knew neither mist nor rain that day, but lay in the light of the evening sun, like islands of the blessed, all their barrenness softened into tenderness as if no storms had ever riven their grim rocks and arid cliffs.

All the way from Rodel to Lochmaddy there was a glorious westering sun. As we drew into the great bay, past the Maddies, Skye lay in the light of the sunset, its cliffs and headlands steeped in a pink mist. Over the low dark lands of Lochmaddy itself the sun was

MACLEOD'S TOMB, RODIL CHURCH

sinking, the molten ball making the myriad wavelets glitter with golden laughter. The sky was cloudless, and the sunset radiance melted upwards into a green glory which was lost in the deep blue zenith above. When at last the sun dipped, the islands became a deep purple. One little level cloud of gold floated in the sky. The very houses and the masts of the *Claymore* lying alongside of us at the pier were glorified against the sensitive heavens. The memory of many a Hebridean night moves me like an old romance, and no pen can ever describe the haunting sense of beauty that rose within us as we watched the dying of one of these ethereal days among the Western Isles.

By ten o'clock a great crowd of people had gathered on the pier alongside the two steamers. In such a place and at such an hour the whole life of the islands unfolds itself. Friends coming and going, meetings and partings, luggage derricks swinging to the rattle of the donkey engines ; the whistle of the busy mate, or the shout of a deck-hand to the men who are working in the dim-lit hold far below. A piper was playing merrily on deck, as the sheep and cattle and provisions were shipped or unloaded. An old *cailleach*—a great-grandmother, in a black bonnet—sat silent on a box and nursed a tiny baby, the young mother and the grandmother beside her—four generations on the pier-head ! —the pang of parting on their faces, while around them arose the merry shouts and laughter of the young folks who were now dancing to the piper. A rosy-faced man in a blue bonnet and a kilt, intent on nothing but his own merchandise ; a set of wild-looking tinkers from Rodel ; bread and drink for the isles, as the deck-hands work unconcernedly at their heavy tasks, and the sound of soft voices tell their heart-tales to each other in the

Gaelic tongue that is older than history. Over all this
traffic of the West, with its mingling of the lonely
shielings and the far-off city to which these soft-
tongued, warm-hearted Celts are returning—the blue-
black sky, the heavenly afterglow, and the watching of
the first stars !

O island hearts ! so sensitive to every mood of the
sky and sea, to the gloom of storms and the laughter of
the sunshine, to the pipe and dance, and the ties of home
which none can cut without a pang—our hearts go out
to you in the love which always understands. We share
your tears when the old lament rises with its piercing
sobs, and we join in your laughter round the fire when
you throw on another peat. May the fires of your
little black houses never go out.

The star of evening, like a little lamp of God, was
hanging in the velvet sky when the afterglow died away.
It cast a long silver thread of light across the sea of
glass. When at midnight we made for Skye again, all
the heaven was strewn with stars. With a wash of seas
about us we moved once more through a world of
mystery, with a prayer in the heart for every island
home that was hushed to slumber beneath the loom of
the hills.

HARRIS FROM BERNERA

VI

THE MAN OF SILENCE

A RAINBOW DAY IN THE FOREST

THERE are days, even in the month of June, when the November-like darkness and a downpour of rain compel a sentimental Scot, whose lot is cast in the haar-haunted city, to manufacture his own sunshine. I suppose the saints could always rise above their surroundings. Those mythical saints! But surely Amiel hit the mark of average humanity when he wrote in his *Journal Intime* that every day is a mood of the soul.

On a day of summer dool like this my heart always goes out to the shining West, and I am thankful that when I close my eyes I only then begin to see. After a summerless June, when we are beginning to wonder if we shall ever see the sun again, I delight to think that on many a western isle the grass is burnt brown on the machairs by the sea because of the long drought and the incessant heat.

.   .   .   .   .   .

It was one of those mornings which were too good to last. Summer was dead. The brackens were beginning to splash the hill-sides with spots of russet and gold. Skye was steeped in sunshine from Hunish Head to the Point of Sleat.

The Coolins rose sharp and clear against the brilliant sky, and the snowy clouds were banked on the horizon

33   C

with a hint of coming showers. In the early morning
the sea had been like glass, and the white clouds repeated
themselves in the mirror of the waters.

But, later on, a breeze sprang up, and the glassy sea
became one vast expanse of the deepest sapphire.

The white boat was waiting on the edge of the tide,
with Donald Mhor tinkering at the engine.

Mike and I stepped on board, and we were soon
racing over the blue seas against the wind and tide,
with a splash of white spray between us and the sun.
We passed Saucy Mary's castle on our way from
Kyleakin to Kylerhea.

On such a morning of dazzling beauty the view up
Loch Alsh to Duich and the Five Sisters of Kintail is
beyond words. But the talk was more of velvet-free
horns than of scenery, for Mike was after the first stag
of the season, and we fervently hoped that for once
Beinn na Cailleach would be free from vagueing
tourists.

True to its over-brightness, the morning broke down,
and just before we reached the old pier on the Skye side
of Kylerhea the first shower swept over us. Mackinnon
the stalker met us at the jetty. He was a middle-aged
man, with a serious weather-beaten face and a white
moustache. There was not an ounce of superfluous flesh
on him. There he stood in the rain, silent and alert,
quite oblivious to anything but the guns, the luncheon
bag, and the work on hand. Weatherwise, and dedicated
to deer, he was absolutely detached from the elements
and contemptuous of a shower, as all the islesmen are.

We sheltered for a little in his house, which was once
the ferry inn. Here I straightway began to think of the
quarrel Dr Johnson had with poor Boswell on the mainland yonder when they were climbing the wild zigzags

of Ratagan before they reached Glenelg—that damp and
dirty inn which was furnished with not a single article
which they could eat or drink. I dreamed also of the
high revels which must have taken place in this gaunt
parlour, where we were now sheltering, when this old
road was the only way from Skye to the southern
markets. The room was immediately filled with a
rabble of phantom drovers and herds, and the sound
of lowing cattle and baa-ing sheep came in at the
window.

Then we set off up the old grass-grown road which
climbs the glen above the Kylerhea river, and joins the
Broadford road at Lusa Bridge, seven miles farther on.
Just where the burn comes tumbling down from Coire
an Fraoich, between Beinn Bhuidhe and Scuir na Coinneach, Mackinnon left the road, and we followed. Here
the real business of the day began, and from that moment
silence was the order of our going.

I still maintain that few town-dwellers have ever been
quite alone, or know what real silence means. But a
hill-man is bred to silence, and a stalker lives on it.
From eleven o'clock until the evening of that day we
climbed and scrambled and spied without any rest,
unless for the half-hour we spent over lunch. During
that time Mackinnon was so intent on the stalk that he
never spoke, only giving an occasional wave of direction
with his arm, or pointing out the slot of a deer with his
stick. As every stalker knows, there are comparatively
few deer on Skye, and no forests of importance ; so the
very intensity of Mackinnon's silence was all the more
humorous.

We climbed to the tops, and crept round Scuir na
Coinneach, Beinn na Greine, and Beinn na Cailleach
itself ; squelching through bogs ; skirting some quite

respectable precipices ; and, on one occasion, slithering
damply down a little waterfall—only pausing when
Mackinnon wished to have another spy through his
long telescope. Sometimes he kneeled and steadied
his glass on his stick. Sometimes he lay down on his
back, and wriggled his leg round the telescope, twisting
his body into every conceivable tortuosity. But there
were no stags !

From the top of Beinn na Greine we saw a motor-
car party having lunch by the side of the old road far
below in the glen, while a dog ranged wildly after some
of the picnickers.

" Good-bye to any chance of a stag on this side of
the glen ! " I whispered to Mike.

Mackinnon glared, waved his hand contemptuously
in the direction of the tourists, shook his head, but
never spoke. It was his way of saying unspeakable
things. The man of silence then determined to leave
the western side of the stalk severely alone, and immediately made over the hill for another beat. We did all
the corries on the north side, but still without picking
up a beast.

Suddenly we noticed a group of sheep, all bunched
together, and moving hurriedly over the ptarmigan
ground on the summit. They stopped and looked back
as if they had been disturbed by something moving
beyond the ridge. But here we drew a blank again,
only marking one blue hare.

It must not, however, be supposed that the day was
dull or inglorious. A fisherman who has trudged home
with an empty basket will know what I mean. The
viewpoints were wonderful. With the scudding showers
and the blazing sun the day was a dream of blue-grey
distances. The circle of vision began with the hills that

rise above Loch Eishort. Rhum lay far out at sea, with a puff of white mist on its peaks, making it true to its name, the Altar Isle of the Sea. Loch Slapin slept in sunshine, with mighty Blaven keeping sentinel, and the Coolins were capped with clouds. The great moors behind Broadford lay like a well-laid carpet of purples and browns, dappled in light and shade. The little Isle of Pabbay floated on the inner seas, green as an emerald. Then the eye ranged from Raasay and Rona across to Torridon, Applecross and Lochcarron, Loch Alsh, Loch Duich, with little Loch Long, the Five Sisters of Kintail, Ben Screel frowning above Loch Hourn—the whole panorama is unequalled in Scotland, and on such a day one dreams of heaven, and wonders if it will be half so beautiful! To remember such a view on the dark November days is to thank God for the vision, the silence, and the beauty of the high tops. For,

> Who has the hills for friend
> Has a God-speed to end
> His path of lonely life,
> And wings of golden memory to depart.
> G. W. YOUNG.

While we were at lunch Mackinnon removed to a distance to brood over his disappointments, so for half an hour we were free to eat and talk and smoke without feeling guilty. I was just waxing eloquent on the tenderness of a well-cooked stag's liver when Mackinnon wandered over to us and quietly lifted the bag with the determined look of a crusader on his face. With the shortest possible number of words he was off again, and, when he led, what could anyone do but follow?

The showers broke on us again and again. The rain tasted cold on the heights, and rainbows made the western world of sea and mountain a perfect fairyland when the sun blazed out again. Mackinnon was spying on the ledge of a little precipice, and we two sat behind a bluff on the steep face sheltering from the stinging rain. When the shower passed, the most glorious double rainbow of the day was thrown across the corrie, enclosing in its arch the whole of Kintail. Mike and I were spellbound, for it was the most vivid display of the spectrum we had ever seen. But Mackinnon rose slowly from his perch and deliberately turned his back on the rainbow! He had seen it without a doubt, as indeed he saw everything. But there was something grand about this silent man giving his whole soul to his work. Beauty was well enough in its way. But his one duty was to find a stag for his young master, and nothing in heaven or on earth would turn him aside from his purpose.

So we continued all day, without resting, following Mackinnon, saying nothing, but wondering how this man of silence would feel in the noise of a midland town, or in the crush of a Rugby International at Murrayfield. I can see the picture distinctly at this moment—the silent Celt with the all-seeing blue eyes walking catlike across the rocks with the rifle in its case over his shoulder; the young sportsman following, tireless, and as keen as youth can be; while the looker-on in a draigled kilt brought up the rear.

When at last we got down in the evening light to the shepherd's cottage at Rhu na Cailleach, Mackinnon turned round, and with perfect courtesy made his first speech of the day :

" I am very sorry, sir, that you have had a blank day."

That was all. But what else was there to say ?

Donald Mhor was waiting for us in the white boat.

" What luck ? " he cried.

" Two big stags," was the modest reply.

" Yes," added Mackinnon, becoming eloquent for the first time, " and you are to be here at seven o'clock to-morrow morning to go up to the top with me to bring down the big stags to the boat."

" Well, well, well," replied Donald Mhor, his heart sinking at every word, " the doctor has brought you the good luck after all."

But he was a sailor man, and the thought of climbing up the steep sides of Beinn na Cailleach in the morning to drag down two heavy stags took all the pleasure out of him.

Next morning, however, there were fifteen deer feeding quietly in the part of the forest which we did not spy. Mike made no mistake, and took the stag in the right place. Not many days after that, I was sitting at home in the haar-haunted city eating delicious stag's liver, with a vision of the man who turned his back on the rainbow, and a wish that this noisy world of chatterers would learn a lesson of silence from him and get on with their work.

VII

THE BORERAIG BAGPIPE

A PIPER'S PILGRIMAGE

It matters not whether you play like MacCrimmon himself or like a travelling tinker, if there is a touch of
Gaelic in the tune and the true swing in the music, you
will get a welcome from a Highland heart in any part
of the world.

To-day the frost is white on the Lowland fields, and
it is a far cry from Auld Reekie to Boreraig. But you
have only to put a tune on the chanter, and yonder is
Dunvegan Loch sleeping in the sun, with the scent of
thyme in the warm winds as you tread the springy turf
of the MacCrimmons' parade ground on the Hoe above
the sea. Then, peace and war, love and hate, and the
hundred thousand battles of the sad old days come
marching down the corridors of time. For, from first
to last, the piob mhor has set the youkie feet of youth
adancing, or sobbed out its coronachs of sorrow—the
friend of man in his deeps of dool or his jaunts of brave
adventure.

We had come a long way, as every piping loon must,
to make the pilgrimage to Boreraig and little Galtrigal.
It was a radiant day.

Many a man has asked me why the day is always so
fine when I make my way through the haunted glens.
And I answer in the word of the old Gaelic saying, " On

the fine day take your coat with you, but on the bad day
go as you please," which means that the fine days live
with us for ever, but the bad days are soon forgot.

So, by Bracadale and Skinidin and Colbost we
travelled, until we were beneath the shadow of Macleod's Tables. Dunvegan, hoary with a thousand years
of history, stood in the sun across the loch. At Husabost, among the smiling crofts, we thought of Alexander
Nicolson—for that great son of Skye was born here—
and we passed along the road singing his immortal
song :

> Jerusalem, Athens, or Rome,
>   I would see them before I die ;
> But I'd rather not see any one of the three
>   Than be banished for ever from Skye.

Then comes the Dun of Boreraig, with Boreraig
itself, and the Piper's Cave at Galtrigal a little way
along the shore.

This ground is sacred to every piper. The site of
MacCrimmon's College is down in that hollow by the
shore. On the long flat Hoe above it the pipers used
to parade when playing, flinging their pibrochs across
the water, while their eyes gazed enraptured on the
incomparable view of the Hebrides, far out beyond
the loch.

Far be it from me to mar my memory of that day
with dates and details of history which every piper
knows. It is enough to say that the greatest of all the
MacCrimmons was Patrick Mor, who succeeded his
father as hereditary piper to the Macleods of Dunvegan. It is impossible to say when the MacCrimmon
family came to Skye ; but tradition says that Alastair
Crotach gave the MacCrimmons their lands at Boreraig ; and Alastair was chief from 1480 to 1540.

Moreover, there are entries in the estate accounts at Dunvegan of payments being made to the MacCrimmons up to the end of the eighteenth century.

What piping must have been heard down there in the hollow, and up here on the Hoe, during these centuries ! To the College at Boreraig came pipers from all parts of Scotland to learn the perfect art—MacArthurs, Mackays, and Campbells. Patrick Mor, like all great musicians, put the secrets of his heart into his playing. His music sprang from his own sobs, as when he composed the " Lament of the Children " after seven of his eight sons died of the fever in one year. So has it been with all great pipers—the bagpipe was their *amchara* or soul-friend. Into it they sobbed their griefs, and out of it came the music of all their battle passions, their love tragedies, and their brave adventures. It would be easy to illustrate this from many of the MacCrimmon masterpieces. And yet, these geniuses had no musical notation such as we use to-day. They used *canntaireachd*, a kind of musical shorthand made up of pronounceable vocables, each of which conveyed a definite note or grace-note which could be crooned to an air.

Sitting on the Hoe at Boreraig I could almost hear the long, heart-breaking notes of the lament—*Cha till mi tuille*, " I return no more," floating down the wind. Piping to these men was a matter of life and death.

In a fit of jealousy an old Breadalbane piper caught hold of the hand of his brother piper and thrust it into the fire to prevent him becoming a better piper than himself.

The MacCrimmons, who kept all the secrets of their system in their own family, once heard that a girl friend had obtained knowledge of a certain combination of notes and passed the information on to her sweetheart. There was only one way of preventing such a leakage of musical information in the future, so the girl's fingers were cut off.

These things are brought strangely near to me. For, as I write, I am fingering a very ancient, home-made, single-handed chanter which was dug up in a peat-bog near the Chief's house in a glen of bloody memories, and I often wonder, when I handle it, if it did not belong to some one-handed piper who in desperation shaped this rude chanter for his remaining hand !

But pleasanter than these is the legend of the Silver Chanter, which has been told in different forms. A great piping competition was taking place at Dunvegan before Macleod. Naturally the Dunvegan piper was to play last. But, when the playing was nearly over, MacCrimmon was nowhere to be found. Calling one of the MacCrimmon lads to him, the Chief sent him to search for the King of Pipers. But, when found, the great MacCrimmon was drunk. Macleod, in despair, then whispered into the boy's ear, " The eleventh piper is just stepping forward, but you will be the twelfth for your Chief." The lad ran out to the hill-side in an agony of consternation. Suddenly a fairy appeared to him from a mound, and presenting him with a silver chanter bade him play. The lad did so, and the little glen at Dunvegan was filled with the divinest piping. Entering the hall when the eleventh piper was just finishing, the MacCrimmon lad put the silver chanter to his lips and outplayed them all.

But piping was not confined to the Highlands of Scotland. We know that the miller in Chaucer's " Canterbury Tales " rode on a horse, playing a

bagpipe with one enormous drone, if the Ellesmere
Manuscript is to be trusted :

> A baggpype wel coude he blowe and sowne,
> And ther-with-al he broghte us out of towne.

Shakespeare speaks of " the drone of a Lincolnshire
bagpipe " and of people who " laugh like parrots at a
bagpiper." Indeed, it may be news to an Englishman
that the bagpipe was an established institution in the
life of old England. From the accounts of the Lord
High Treasurer we learn that the English bagpipers
used to visit the Scots Court, for on 10th July 1489 there
is an entry for payment, " eight shillings to Inglis pyparis
that came to the castle yet and playit to the king."

Stranger still, William of Wykeham in 1403 presented New College, Oxford, with a silver gilt Pastoral
Staff, exquisitely wrought and bejewelled. It is one of
the most gorgeous relics of its kind, and is usually kept
in a glazed recess on the north side of the chapel. If
you look carefully at this ancient crozier you will notice
among the many figures carved on it an angel playing
the bagpipes.

Strangest of all, perhaps, is Holbein's drawing (No.
47) in his famous series called " The Dance of Death."
Here the Fool is mocking Death by putting his finger
in his mouth, and at the same time is endeavouring to
strike him. Death smiles and is amused at his efforts,
and leads him away in a dancing attitude, playing all
the time on a bagpipe which has a chanter and two
large drones.

But, indeed, the bagpipe is mentioned in history and
literature all down the centuries. From Giraldus Cam-
brensis in the twelfth century, through the writings of
James I., William Dunbar, John Knox, and many others,

the bagpipe drones its way. Only in Aberdeen, " that unnatural town," as Samuel Rutherford called it, did the Magistrates prohibit the common piper from going his rounds on 26th May 1630, " it being an uncivil forme to be usit within sic a famous burghe and being often fund fault with."

The most unique bagpipe I ever saw lies in the Museum at Naples. There, among the tragic relics which were found in the buried city of Pompeii, you will find a bagpipe with two little drones and a very small bag, all fossilised, as it had lain for centuries in that lava-covered city. And yet we need not be surprised at bagpipes in Pompeii, for a bagpipe appears on one of the Roman coins of Nero's time.

Every man must be allowed to make his own notes on the history of anything. So, even when sitting in the sun on the Hoe at Boreraig, my thoughts flew to a collection of photographs of monkish misereres which I possess.

The word " miserere " was at first applied to the Penitential 51st Psalm, which commences with the words " *Miserere mei, Domine.*" Later on the word was applied to the wooden seat in a chancel stall on which the monk sat. Hinges were put on in later times, so that the monk, when he stood up to sing the long service or the penitential psalms, could rest himself on the bulged edge when the seat was hinged back against the stall. On the wood, just below the bulged edge, was invariably carved the grotesque figure of a beast or man. So in the old pre-Reformation cathedrals, abbeys, and churches, these miserere seats provide a humorous instance of how the weary but wily monks managed to sit during a long service when they were supposed to be standing. And who will blame them ?

Hinge up these ancient seats, and what will you find ? Under one miserere in Beverley Minster a monkey is playing a bagpipe while a bear dances. Under another, in the same church, a pig plays the pipes at the pig trough, while two little pigs look on. A third seat in Beverley shows a monkey imitating a piper by holding a dog inverted under the arm, seizing the hind legs with both hands, and putting the dog's tail in the mouth for a chanter—all to the utter consternation of the dog, which snarls behind the monkey's back. In Ludlow Church a headless demon carries a dishonest pothouse woman to hell to the accompaniment of the bagpipe, and at the other end of the miserere you see her actually disappearing into the pit. In Ripon Cathedral there is a miserere under which is carved a well-groomed pig, with a shingled mane, playing the pipes, to the evident delight of two piglets that gaze entranced at the player. Even when we leave the misereres the bagpipe motive follows us to the carving on wooden screens and the stone sculptured architecture of the cathedral itself. In Exeter Cathedral there is a fine screen in front of the Minstrels' Gallery, with twelve angels playing twelve different musical instruments. The second angel on the left is playing a bagpipe—a sure sign that the music of the pipes was considered to be of heavenly origin ! Last of all, high up on the south wall of our own Melrose Abbey there is a gargoyle in the form of a very straight-nosed pig playing the pipes.

From all which we infer that the monks of the Middle Ages, on both sides of the Border, were well acquainted with the bagpipe, that they were humorists of the first water, that the pig was a favourite subject, and that the ancient pipe had only one drone.

When I think of the dog, on the miserere at Beverley, being used by the monkey as a bagpipe, I am reminded of a saying in the Highlands, " There's both meat and music here," said the dog when he ate the piper's bag. And of still another old word, which is surely not of Highland origin, " Bring not a bagpiper to a man in trouble."

Whilst sitting in the blessed sunshine of Boreraig that day, I saw an old man cutting hay with a scythe on a croft close by. The only sound that broke the silence was the rasp of the old man's hone on his antique scythe. Eleven sweeshes in the lush grass, and the mower paused to rest. Other eleven sweeshes, and he looked about him again. I counted the rhythmic strokes, and the resting times seemed to grow longer at every pause. Here, surely, was the peace, the leisure, and the dreaming memories of a life from which the adventure had long since fled. Then I looked at the site of the famous piping college by the shore. The old man was a parable of what had been and would never be again. Had not I seen MacCrimmon's pipes lying in a case at Dunvegan ? The wail of his own lament seemed to be wafted across the loch on the warm winds that whispered about the ears :

Cha till mi tuille . . . I come again
no more.

VIII

THE FINEST ROAD IN SKYE

FROM KYLE TO DUNVEGAN

IF I had but one day to spend in Skye, and only one road to travel, I am in no doubt about what that road would be. In this age of hurry people are taking their pleasures in tabloid form. I suppose it is inevitable. Crowds arrive at Kyle every summer day and look across the narrow strait waiting for the ferry to carry them over the sea to Skye. Whether they bring cars with them or only a stout stick and a rucksack, their only thought is to see as much of the magic Isle as they can in the shortest possible time. I do not blame them. For one glimpse of the Coolins, even from a distance, sanctifies a summer, as the sight of a lover's face will always be worth a whole day's journey.

But let none think that they will ever surprise the secrets of Skye in that way. Even those of us who have known the island for the best part of a lifetime, sailed its sea lochs, walked its lonely roads, and stood on its highest pinnacle, are still waiting for a longer acquaintance before we can begin to set down our tale of love. But the best love stories in the world will never be written.

Kyleakin is the doorstep of Skye. You are no sooner in the ferry-boat than you are gazing at a little row of white cottages on the farther shore. Westward, up the Kyle, the lighthouse gleams on its island, with the dim

THE COOLIN RIDGE FROM BRUACH NA FRITHE

blue hills beyond. Eastward, down the Kyle, lies Loch Alsh with its glorious tumble of hills. Right in front of you stands the ruin of Castle Moil on its rock. This keep was built by a Danish Princess—Saucy Mary, the sailors called her, for she stretched a chain across the Kyle and took toll of every ship that passed. For centuries the Mackinnons owned it.

Kyleakin is the pleasantest of all the Skye villages. But, however fair the doorstep may be, it is not the whole house. It may seem but a commonplace row of cottages from the mainland, but the finest thing about Kyleakin, with its green machair and its little tidal ob, is the view out of it. You are no sooner out of the village and across the ravine of the Alt Anavaig, on the road to Broadford, than the Coolins rise before you far away across the little moss haggs of the moor. At Lusa Bridge the old coach road to Kylerhea turns off to the left—a fine six-mile walk for a summer day. Then for some miles you pass through the prosperous townships of Breakish, and you are at Broadford with the Red Hills rising before you.

I never pass through Broadford but I think of Samuel Johnson at Coirechatachan, and Alexander Smith at the Cattle Fair.

The ruins of Coirechatachan lie across the river beneath Ben na Cailleach, one of the Red Hills. A poor rickle of stones now, but once the hospitable home of Mackinnon, who was Johnson's host. Here Boswell got drunk on the Saturday night, and brought down on himself Johnson's heavy rebuke. But there was more than drink going at Coirechatachan. For, later on, Johnson was seen whispering to Corrie's wife, who immediately cried out : " Oh, I am in love with him ! " After which the great man kissed her hand.

D

Then one of the married ladies in the company actually sat on Johnson's knee, put her arms round his neck, and kissed him.

" Do it again," said he, " and let us see who will tire first ! "

If poor Bozzy's head could not stand the Highland whisky, what of Dr Johnson, who, when he was in Edinburgh, drank nineteen cups of tea in the house of Dr Blacklock, the blind poet, much to the consternation of his hostess ! Skye is full of the reminiscences of his visit. Over yonder in Raasay he was particularly happy, and on the top of Duncaan, Boswell danced a reel with the rest.

Just a little way down the Ardvasar road, at the Market Stance of Strolamus, Alexander Smith, the author of the finest book on Skye, once attended a cattle fair with his host, young M'Ian of Ord. When M'Ian and he were driving off at the end of the day they came on John Kelly, one of the Ord shepherds, snoring in the heather. Nothing could rouse him.

" We must take him on his fighting side," said M'Ian, whose knowledge of human nature was infinite.

So he shouted into John's ear, " Here's a man from Kyle who says he's a better man than you."

" Tell him to strike me," growled the shepherd.

" Kick him as hard as you can," whispered M'Ian to Smith. And Smith kicked.

John sat up instantly and struck out.

" Catch him now ; his rage has sobered him ; he'll be drunk next minute ; get him into the dog-cart at once."

And this is how they got John Kelly of the childlike heart home.

While wandering about the fair, Smith remembered

Johnson's visit to Coirechatachan, and set out alone to visit the shrine. He never reached it, but mistook another ruin for it. But, what does it matter ? These three men—Samuel Johnson, James Boswell, and Alexander Smith—by their inimitable writings, were the first who really made Skye a famous place of pilgrimage, and their ghosts haunt the island still.

The way from Broadford to Sligachan is now made easy for the most fastidious motorist by the new road which skirts the shore from Dunan to Sconser. It is all very smooth and of an easy gradient. But only those who have trudged up the old steep road, across the hills from Dunan to Luib on Loch Ainort, and then from Kinloch Ainort through the wilds of Lord Macdonald's forest beneath the gloom of Glamaig to Sconser Lodge at the mouth of Loch Sligachan, can ever appreciate the solitude and grandeur of this region.

At Sconser may still be seen one or two black houses, with the peat reek coming from the wooden chimney in the thatched roof and through the open door. On the roof of one of these black houses I once saw a man sitting, idly contemplating the universe, after the manner of the Celt. For the roof was simply a continuation of the hill-side, like so many of the old black houses I used to see in Harris thirty years ago. It was at Sconser Inn that the island chiefs met Clanranald, Prince Charlie's messenger, in 1745. But, to the consternation of the Jacobites, Macleod would not " come out."

The little fisherman's hut at the burn-mouth before you come to Dunan is an ideal cabin made of wood, with a stone-built fireplace. It always reminds me of the hut in which Thoreau wrote his " Walden." Here might a solitary live in peace, think high thoughts, and live on sea trout.

The glorious colour of the sea wrack at the head of
Loch Ainort when the tide is far out, great stretches of
ochres and umbers and madders, with splashes of bright
green sea grass, make a perfect painter's palette on the
shores of this lonely little loch.

There is a beautiful view of Raasay House and the
open Sound from this point, with a glimpse of the Old
Man of Storr far away to the north. It seems like a
millennium of years since I first sailed up that Sound,
with the fresh breeze filling the white sails and never a
flutter at the leech.

To-day the whole of Skye is clear of clouds. But
I remember a day here when I saw the searchlight of
the sun piercing the lowering clouds and sending its
spotlight racing along the gloomy hill-side. At the end
of the loch there is an old *caraidh*, or fish weir, which
is a horse-shoe curve of stones set in the shallow water
to catch the fish when the tide recedes. You will find
remains of these primitive fish dams all round the shores
of Skye. A packman, carrying his whole stock-in-trade
on his back, is trudging along with the natural solemnity
of one who has more time for meditation than the
average shopman of the towns.

To lovers of Skye Sligachan means—the Coolins
hemming you in with all their silent mystery ; Glamaig
and little Marsco for ever in your eye, with Scuir nan
Gillean at the back door ; the old grey bridge over the
Sligachan river, which tumbles down the glen eternally ;
rain and mist ; and the burning heat of a summer sun
when all the world of islands and seas is spread below
you like the map of God, as you stand on the summit
rocks and gaze spellbound.

There are no facilities at Sligachan for the towny
tourist. It will never become a motoring centre. The

ROAD TO THE COOLINS, SKYE

atmosphere of the Inn suggests nothing but ice-axes and fishing-rods, and the comfortable peace of wise men who linger long in this climbers' paradise to exercise their natural gifts of mind and muscle.

No man knows Skye who does not know the Coolins. They draw the eye from almost every Hebridean isle, and get at the heart of mountain lovers as no other hills in Britain ever will. Whether you have the skill to climb their beetling rocks, or only wander round the corries which seem to be bastioned by the walls of the primeval world, or approach them from Loch Scavaig or Loch Brittle, or penetrate the sanctuaries from Sligachan itself, the Coolins must ever remain the preserve of man in all the glory of his strength.

When you leave Sligachan, instead of going north to Portree by Glen Varragill, keep straight on past the end of the Inn on the road that leads to the west. The jagged ridges of the Coolins are soon left behind, and the green moors of Drynoch are all about you, dappled with cloud and sunshine. Grassy Drynoch of the fine sheep walks is a great contrast to the wilderness about Sligachan. But, that is Skye. A place of sudden changes and great contrasts. From rain to sunshine, from cloudy gloom to heavenly radiance, from the uttermost desolation to the greenest hills. Over the face of this dearest of islands mist and sunlight chase each other like laughter and tears on the face of a little child.

Yonder across Loch Harport is the Talisker Distillery. I can still hear as in a dream the lilting voice of the Highlander describing the triple process of distilling to some American friends as we wandered from vat to vat. But the refrain was always the same—" And the third time it is whuskey ! " That is all I picked up about the making of whisky, and still in my sleepless hours, when I lie and think of Skye, I hear only one sound on the winds of Carbost—" And the third time it is whuskey."

Is there any sea loch in Skye that can sparkle with more heavenly laughter after rain than Loch Bracadale ? If it is a blue day when you pass that way you will see the Hebrid Isles lying like clouds on the rim of the ocean, and great beauty lying over Bracadale, with the Isles of Wiay, Tarner, and Harlosh floating like Viking ships in the bay. Macleod's Tables dominate the landscape to the west, and Macleod's Maidens stand up in the sea at the Point of Idrigil. Huge headlands guard the entrance to the loch. To landward the low green hills are dotted with sheep and cattle. It is all crofts, peat reek, yellow sands, and red wrack round these tidal shores.

The ruins of the broch—Dun Beag—stand near Struan. Dr Johnson, when staying at Ulinish, visited this dun and enlarged on the fact that in Skye " there is an ambition of exalting whatever has survived memory." He also recorded the fact that " Mr Boswell caught a cuddy." The little children of Skye were laughing at their play when we passed the sunny hayfields of Struan. But the brave sons of Skye who have made the traditions of the Misty Isle are scattered to the ends of the earth, and sleep soundly in their foreign graves. No more for them the scent of the peat reek or the sound of the wintry seas.

At the head of Loch Caroy we boiled the kettle, and sat by the roadside near the derelict chapel of St John the Baptist. This plain little Episcopal chapel by the side of the tree-clad ravine always intrigues me, for it seems to speak of an alien faith in a strange land. The seats are all gone. The windows are in a perilous state.

A white cross lies across what must have been a simple altar. Even the graves outby record the names of alien sojourners who worshipped God after the manner of their forefathers—Scott, Porteous, Gibbon. Now the wall is crumbling. There is a padlock on the gate. The grass is all tangled, and the trees are overgrown. When I came out again the tide had receded in the little loch. Ichabod ! Here, too, is a tale that has been told.

It is not far from the Caroy burn to Dunvegan. You have scarcely left the last waters of Bracadale at Pool Roag when you see Dunvegan Loch airting out to the sunset. The castle is the Mecca of all who come to Skye. But Dunvegan is so great a sight that it brooks no mere mention at the end of a traveller's story. So the long day's journey must end in the old Kirkyard of Kilmuir at Dunvegan.

Here is the burial-place of the chiefs of Macleod— fit resting-place for so great a succession. It stands on a hill with a wide view of the Tables, a burn whimpling past, spleenworts in the ruined walls, and a multitude of sad old graves. Conspicuous among them is the Lovat pyramid, raised in memory of Thomas Lord Lovat, who married a Macleod. He was the father of the notorious M'Shimi of the 'Forty-five, and he died in 1699. The inscription, which is now almost obliterated, drew forth a sneer from Dr Johnson, who said it was " poor stuff, such as Lord Lovat's butler might have written."

But all opinions seem small when we wander among the graves of dead men, and when the sun goes down the day's cares are soon forgotten.

IX

SLEAT-OF-THE-WAVES

THE GARDEN OF SKYE

THERE are a great many Gaelic proverbs about Sleat, and, strange to say, most of them are about women! Russet Sleat of the Fine Women; Sleat Wives Worth Having; Sleat of the Talkative Ones. These are a few. Even Duncan Ban, who got his wife from Sleat, speaks proudly of her as being of the seed of the Sleat dwellers. I suppose it means that the merits of any district depend largely on its womenfolks. Or is it something else? Be that as it may, Sleat is a pleasant place of low hills, green fields, bird-haunted woods, and sheltered shores. When you take the road to Sleat, you turn your back on the wild region of the Coolin and your face to a fair-favoured land.

The Ardvasar road strikes due south a little east of Broadford, and crosses a region of great moors. Water lilies float like snowflakes on the blue waters of the Lochan Dubh, and as you look across the black tarns these rare blooms seem all the more beautiful because they are so inaccessible. Here, and later on at Loch nan Dubrachan, the old legend of the Water Horse is called to mind, for in every other Highland loch the dreaded *each uisge* used to appear in the mouth of a winter night when the half-lights of the gloaming made the moors an eerie place to stray in.

As you travel on you catch a glimpse of the head-waters of Loch Eishort, the blue tops of Rhum, and the furrowed brow of Blaven. Nearer at hand the Red Hills dominate the moors. And still the landscape opens out at every mile. Little Lochan-a-Daal, with its red sea wrack and its lodge of Kinloch snuggling beside a bouquet of trees. Isle Ornsay right in front of you. The mainland mountains of Loch Hourn across the Sound, with Ben Screel lording it over the whole landscape. Here are green fields and the delightful gardens of Duisdale House, with prosperous crofts, and farther on, the deep-gladed woods of Armadale. Indeed, the low lands of Sleat, seen from the mainland on a sunny day in harvest time, look as if they were covered with a tartan plaid of green and yellow checks. Little wonder that Sleat-of-the-Waves has been called the Garden of Skye.

Behind Isle Ornsay the sailor can always find good harbourage. It holds many pleasant memories for me. I still remember that our skipper, Captain Mac, called the place R'onsay, and as I had never been there before, I could not remember any place in Skye of that name. Now, long afterwards, I know that his sailor's pro-nunciation of R'onsay was nearer the mark than I then realised. For this island, despite the fact that there are the ruins of an ancient chapel on it, is not named after Saint Oran, like the Island of Oronsay which lies off Colonsay. Both of those islands are called after saints —Colonsay after Columba and Oronsay after Oran. But the word Ornsay is a place description pure and simple. The island is called in Gaelic Eilean Diarmid or Diarman, which easily becomes Eilean Tiarman, a corruption of Eilean Tioram or Dry Island. Now, *tioram* is the Gaelic equivalent for the Norse word *oras-ey*, which means Ebb-tide Island. So Isle Ornsay is the island that is connected with the mainland at low tide—a very exact description of the place. A long rigmarole about Isle Ornsay, doubtless, but it all goes to show that " unto him that hath shall be given "— although even a saint should not have more islands called after him than he has a right to.

I can well remember an excursion that June night to a croft on the Ardvasar road, in order to buy a hen. We did buy one, but we had to take it away alive, as there was none at the croft at that moment who could thraw the neck of the poor creature. So I carried the living hen with some trouble into Isle Ornsay post office, and there, while I was transacting business with the postmistress, the hen ran off. There was great cackling in the village street that evening, and the race was not altogether to the swift. So small a thing will linger in the memory for a lifetime when greater things are altogether forgotten.

The road cuts inland across a purple tongue of land for three or four miles, and joins the sea again at Knock Bay and the prosperous township of Teangue. This is just the old Norse word *tunga*, so well known in Sutherland as Tongue. Here, on a little rocky knoll by the sea, stands the ivy-covered ruin of Knock Castle, sometimes called Castle Camus. This keep was for a long time a residence of the Macdonalds of the Isles. In the reign of James IV the Macleods laid siege to it, but the siege was raised by a brave woman of Clan Donald, who was ever after called Mairi 'Caistiel. Like all ancient keeps, Castle Camus was haunted. The gruagach's stone is still pointed out, but in this case the *glastig*, or Green Lady, turned out to be a she-devil who appeared in the form of a grey goat.

Another mile and you reach one of the holy shrines of Skye—the old ruined Kirk of Sleat, which is called Kilmore. Surely the war memorial of Sleat has an unrivalled stance on the green knoll near the kirk, with an outlook across the waters of the Sound to the mountains of Knoydart!

In this old kirkyard I have often lingered. The beauty of the place literally compels you, when the wind blows in from the sea and whispers eternal secrets to you as it rustles through the leaves of the immemorial trees. Close by the ruin stands the new kirk. The whole place is a perfect poem—the vista through the Norman east window, the view of Knoydart and the sea, the ancient monuments of the Macdonalds who lie well happed under the old turf, the tree-embowered road outby, and the song of a robin as it sits in the September sun and chants the low, sad song of man's mortality.

Here, doubtless, long ago there was a pagan place of worship. Thereafter, on the same site, a Celtic monk would set up his little cell of Christ. But the first church was built by a priest called Crotach Mac Ghillie Gorm —the Hunch-backed Son of the Blue Servitor, and a Canon of Beauly. This good man travelled all the way across Scotland to preach Christ to the wild men of Skye. His primitive church stood at Kilmore until some time in the seventeenth century, when the Macleods fought a battle with the MacIntyres in a neighbouring field. When the MacIntyres were defeated, they sought refuge in the church, which, like all churches at that time, had a thatched roof. The Macleods locked the door, set fire to the thatch, and destroyed church, MacIntyres, and all. A second church was built by Macdonald of Sleat in 1691, but, according to Ian

Lom, the Lochaber Bard, the Chief never saw it finished :

> To the church of Sleat-of-the-Waves
> Its cost you defrayed to build,
> Though you did not wait to slate it.

This church was used for worship until 1876, and it is now the most beautiful of all the ruined kirks in Skye.

Armadale Castle is a thing of yesterday. When the guns of Waterloo were silenced, the masons began to build this modern castle of the Macdonalds in Skye.

But it was in a small house at Armadale that Dr Johnson and Boswell were entertained in 1773 by Sir Alexander Macdonald, the first Lord Macdonald of Slate, in the peerage of Ireland (1776). He was a very accomplished man and loved music. Indeed, he composed a number of strathspeys and reels which are still popular, such as " Lord Macdonald's Reel," " Mrs Macleod of Raasay," " Mrs Mackinnon, Corry," etc. He was a first-rate violinist, and on one occasion entertained O'Kane, the celebrated Irish harper, to whom he gave a beautiful old harp key which had been long in his family, and was said to be worth eighty or a hundred guineas. It was " made with gold and silver, and set with a precious stone."

Lord Macdonald was a writer of Latin verses and a member of the Society of Antiquaries. The house in which he lived at Armadale in 1773 was only that of a tenant, because the family mansion had been previously burned. His entertainment may have been very frugal, as, indeed, a scholar's often is. But both Johnson and Boswell abused his hospitality unpardonably by holding up their host to ridicule for his poverty. Johnson

LOCH CORUISK, SKYE

actually complained in a letter to Mrs Thrale " that he had disgusted all mankind by injudicious parsimony " . . . " that he had no cook " . . . and " that Boswell was very angry." Boswell himself, however, makes this illuminating remark in his Journal—" I had felt a return of spleen during my stay at Armadale."

Why was it that these two travellers spoke of their Highland host so ungraciously ? It would almost seem as if Boswell had influenced Johnson against their host. But Dr Johnson did not know what we now know— that Boswell had been an unsuccessful suitor for the hand of Miss Diana Bosville, the very Lady Macdonald who was doing her best to entertain him ! This fact may have accounted for his own acknowledged attack of spleen. Moreover, had Dr Johnson known that, he would probably have restrained himself from foolish taunts, and been a more gracious guest when Bozzy was inclined to be nasty at Armadale. The remarks of both about their host at Armadale will not be found in any modern edition, as they only appeared in the first editions of the two Journals, and were subsequently omitted as being altogether improper.

The woods of Armadale are now deep-gladed and luxuriant. The great trees stand in park-like lands, and sweep the ancient turf with their green skirts. Auricarias and rhododendrons flourish here. Indeed, you might think you were wandering through an English demesne of sylvan beauty were it not for the fact that the windows of the grey castle of the Macdonalds are winking in the sun at the wild mountains of Nevis across the sparkling seas.

Then comes homely Ardvasar, with its crofts, its bien houses, and its harvest fields. From Ardvasar it is an up-and-down road all the way to the Aird of Sleat,

where a little church stands four-square to every wind
that blows, looking right across the open seas to Eigg
of the Songs and the white sands of Morar. I have lit
my fire on that glamorous road that leads to the end of
everything.

But Ardvasar itself is a place of large leisure. On
one occasion I chapped at the inn door and asked for
tea. A little time after that I saw a woman gathering
sticks to light the fire. So we began to explore the by-
ways of Ardvasar in the sun, when lo ! we found that
the hedgerows were hanging with the most luscious
brambles. To this day I wonder if there are any
brambles in the world so large and succulent.

After tea I smoked a meditative pipe over the inn
library. Among the old books I found the following :
"Calvin's Institutes in Latin." Edited by Tholuck.
Berlin, 1834.

"The Liquor Laws of Scotland." By David
Dewar.

"Historical Collections, Relating to Remarkable
Periods of the Success of the Gospel, and Eminent
Instruments Employed in Promoting it." 1754.

"A Greek Grammar." 1831.

Latin, Greek, Whisky, and Religion—these four
books seemed to form a synopsis of the scholarship, the
conviviality, and the principles of the eighteenth-century
lairds whom Dr Johnson met in Skye. For, despite
Lord Macdonald's poverty, Boswell was good enough
to advertise to the world that the laird of Armadale " had
been an Eton scholar, and being a gentleman of talents,
Dr Johnson had been very well pleased with him in
London."

.   .   .   .   .   .

O Sleat-of-the-Waves. Far away in a city of the

south, when the winter storm thrashes on the window-panes, and the rain-swept streets hold in them no beauty that the eye can see, I sometimes dream of the old ivy-covered Kirk of Sleat at Kilmore, sleeping in the sun-shine among the trees, with the blue waters of the Sound gleaming like the crystal sea betwixt the shores of Skye and the ethereal mountains of Knoydart. And—my heart turns within me.

X

CASTLES IN SKYE

DUNSCAITH: DUNTULM: DUNVEGAN

CASTLES in Skye! The very thought inflames the imagination. A castle in the Hebrides is not like a castle in the south. These ancient castles in Skye— with one exception—are grim ruins standing on rocky cliffs or headlands looking out to sea. Built for defence in the dim days of old, their stark walls defy the storms that rage around their sodden sites, and every stone is lashed by the spindrift that blows like smoke across the tumbling seas. They have been crumbling for centuries; yet, for all their fallen strength, they are the true historians of the Isles, and the legendry of a thousand years blows about their lichened walls like the sough of summer winds.

There are at least fifty Duns in Skye—that is, little rocky mounds which are crowned with the foundations or the ruins of brochs, fortresses, or castles. Even the oldest castle stands on the site of a still older broch or tower. A whole volume could be written about these ruins, and to visit each would entail an arduous journey by land and sea round the whole seaboard of Skye.

But no man can ever get at the real romance of a country by sitting at home and wading through the history books. He must take the road for himself and see all its wonders with his own eyes. If you would surprise the secrets of the isles, the sun and the rain must have kissed your cheeks in many a day's adventure, and the good Gaelic must have sounded in your ears like the overcome of an old song whose ending no man will ever know.

Of all the castles in Skye, the three greatest are Dunscaith, Duntulm, and Dunvegan.

As you travel south from Isle Ornsay, you come to a gate on the right-hand side of the road just beyond Loch nan Dubrachan. Open the gate, and there lies before you a rough road that cuts across the promontory of Sleat for five miles to Ord on Loch Eishort. Here the moors are low-lying and green. After passing Loch Meoble and before coming to the trees on the right the road takes a plunge down a stony hill and then through a tree-clad gorge. Here you get your first view of Blaven. At this spot I met two very large flocks of black-faced sheep, with ten drovers and their dogs, and I immediately thought of old M'Ian, young M'Ian, and Alexander Smith, who must often have passed this way. The road has a desperate surface of rough stones, and there is a great buttress of rock near the sheep fanks. Then comes Ord House, with its little pointed windows, and three dormers in the roof. It is a comfortable homestead standing on a knoll above the sea, and sheltered by a clump of trees.

Ord looks straight to Blaven across the sparkling seas. Here M'Ian, an islesman of the old school and a hardy veteran of the wars, lived with his family in the early days of the nineteenth century. At that time a tacksman in Skye was a kind of Shepherd King. M'Ian was over eighty years of age, of a slight wiry figure, with a fresh complexion and a crown of snow-white hair. As a soldier he had carried colours in Ireland at the end of

E

the eighteenth century. He fought with Moore at Corunna, lifted his gallant leader when he was wounded, and saw the light of pleasure in his dying eyes when the Highlanders charged. He followed Wellington all through the Peninsular Campaign, and was himself wounded at Quatre Bras. At Waterloo he stood in a square that crumbled but never flinched. Then, like countless numbers of old soldiers, M'Ian retired to his beloved Highlands and took a tack of land in Skye. He was a master of legendary lore, an expert genealogist, and an enthusiast in Gaelic poetry. But he was so quick of temper that contradiction drew fire from him like steel from flint. He would let fly a volley of oaths at a careless servant one moment, and the next be bowing his white head most reverently as he knelt at evening prayers. Such was Alexander Smith's hospitable and most human host at Ord. Smith married a M'Ian in 1857, and in 1865 published his " Summer in Skye." My edition (1866) is adorned with a rather crude frontispiece of the " View from M'Ian's House," showing an old boat on the green shore, the blue waters of Loch Eishort, with mighty Blaven rising from the shores of Slapin like a pink and purple cockscomb, and a peep of the blue Coolins beyond.

It was a perfect August day, and the peace of God lay over Skye. The road from Ord to Tokavaig and the old castle of Dunscaith is rough and steep. As I trudged through the woods of hazel and birch, in the sweltering heat, it seemed that every day in this quiet place must be a Sabbath. Here was a world of silence, sleep, and beauty, with but one sound—the far-off bleat of a sheep. This road continues past Dunscaith to the next township of Tarskavaig, and so leads you back across Sleat to Ostaig and Kilbeg on the Sound.

The desolate ruin of Dunscaith stands on a square bluff by the shore. But what seems an innocent-looking bluff from a distance is really an isolated rock on the north side of a little bay called Ob Gauscavaig. This precipitous rock rises forty feet sheer from the sea on three sides. On the landward side it is cut off from access by a deep gully which is spanned by two arched walls over which there must have been at one time a drawbridge. A flight of stone steps turning to the left rises from the end of the bridge and enters the ruined wall of the castle. Crumbling walls, grass-grown foundations, a beetling rock, traces of an old well, and a glorious view seawards—that is what anyone may see at Dunscaith to-day.

But the glamour of the place will only fall over those who know something of the legendry of Fingal and his heroes, for the poetry of Ossian broods over this wild rock like a sea mist that is shot with sunlight.

It is impossible to thread out the various legends which connect Cuchullin with Dunscaith, and one has to choose between many tales. But it is told that Cuchullin came in his youth from Erin over the waves to Dunscaith to learn the arts of war which were taught there by Sgathach the Terrible, who was Queen of Skye. That must have been in the far-off days of Celtic occupation, for it was Columba who first forbade women to fight in battle. This ruthless Princess had five score of warrior women in her college of arms, and these Amazons on one occasion executed fifty sea rovers by tying the long hair of each to the bough of an oak tree. There the miserable men hung till they died. One of these warrior women was Maev the Strong.

Cuchullin fell in love with Sgathach, the beautiful queen of battle whom the Celts called Bragela, which means the Fair Bosomed. Although fierce in warfare, she was passionately fond of music, possessing a three-stringed harp of magical powers—one string being tuned to laughter, a second to weeping, and a third to sleep. Cuchullin called the queen his Tender Tutoress. And indeed she must have been tender as well as terrible, for she loved him dearly, and having that second sight which is always lengthened by love, foresaw his death in Erin.

So Ossian sings : " O strike the harp in praise of my love, the lonely sunbeam of Dunscaith. Strike the harp in praise of Bragela . . . spread now thy white sails for the Isle of Mist and see Bragela leaning on her rock. Her tender eye is in tears, and the winds lift her long hair from her heaving breast. She listens to the winds of night to hear the voice of the rowers, to hear the song of the sea, and the sound of thy distant harp. And long shall she listen in vain. Cuchullin will never return."

O Dunscaith ! What care I though Maclean of Duart or Macdonald of Sleat lived here in later times ! My thoughts always fly back to those dim days when Cuchullin and his heroes sailed in their galleys betwixt Erin and Skye. When Bragela of the Fair Bosom looked in vain across the darkling seas for the hero of her heart who was never to return. Did not Cuchullin chain his hound Luath to yonder stone ? And do the old wrinkled sennachies of Skye not tell you yet that he is hunting with his dogs when the storm roars among the hills ?

" Call," said Fingal, " call my dogs, the long-bounding sons of the chase. Call white-breasted Bran, and the surly strength of Luath."

From Dunscaith to Duntulm is a far cry, and you

DUNVEGAN CASTLE

have to travel the whole length of Skye from Cuchullin's castle till you reach the ancient stronghold of the Macdonalds of the Isles. But every step of the journey brings you some new wonder of beauty or lore.

North of Portree, none but a Londoner will expect a boulevard. But the very roughness of the road secures the peace of the whole seaboard that lies to the east of the great ridge of Trotternish. First come the black splintered precipices of the Storr, with that mighty obelisk which is known as the Old Man of Storr. Only those who have sketched the Old Man from every angle know what a many-sided character he is. The picturesque gorge of Tote, with the now disused Diatomite workings, and the little derelict railway that led to Lealt in the moors. Culnacnock, where the local postman goes his rounds on a long-tailed brown pony, and you can see the level strata of sandstone below the upright pillars of volcanic rock on a little hillock on the right-hand side of the road. Then Staffin Bay, with its lovely sweep of sand, and Staffin Island lying in the lap of the sea. Here there is a multitude of crofts, and the whole world of Staffin is dominated by the gigantic flat table of the Quirang, flanked by its pillared cliffs. It will pay you to turn up the road to Uig and see the old graveyard of Kilmaruy. All the way north there are superb views across the sea to the tumbled mass of the Ross-shire hills, and at Tote there is a fine backward view to the now far-off Coolins. But when you cross the northmost tip of Skye, by Kilmaluag, the outlook suddenly changes and you are gazing westward over the sea to the dim blue hills of Harris, with the rugged ruin of Duntulm Castle standing up on its green hill like a grim sentry in the foreground of the whole panorama.

E 2

This Gaelic word describes Duntulm with complete exactitude :

> Ged tha thu 'n diugh 'a d'aibheas fhuar
> Bha thu uair 'a d'aros righ.

> Though thou art to-day a ruin cold,
> Thou wert once the dwelling of a king.

For Duntulm was the ancient seat of the Macdonalds. Their chiefs were Kings of the Isles, and proudly challenged the reigning Kings of Scotland. But this is not the place to enter upon a genealogy which a per-fervid Macdonald will assure you goes back to that High King of Ireland, Conn of the Hundred Battles, and even to Breogan the twenty-third in descent from Japhet ! That feud is certainly not for my claymore.

Like all these ancient castles, Duntulm was built on the site of a Viking fortress, called Dun Dhaibidh, or the Dun of David, after the hardy Norseman who seized the place. That Norse castle in turn was doubtless built on the site of a still older Celtic fort, and these Celtic forts take us back beyond all the records of history.

Duntulm, true to its name, is *Dun Tulm nam baideal arda*—Duntulm of the High Tower. It is a castle that sits high on a knoll by the sea, with a steep green approach from the landward side, and a fifty-foot drop of rocky cliff to the waves on the other three sides. So it was impregnable from the sea. The usual protecting ditch was cut on the landward side to a depth of fifteen feet, but over this ditch has been raised a broad track in later times to make an easier approach.

It is all a dream of ruined walls, waving grasses, whispering winds, and infinite horizons. The old chamber with the barrel roof, an aumbry at one end and a fireplace at the other. The rugged remains of the old tower. The fascinating view of distant Harris seen through the sea-gate in the northern wall. The little isle of Tulm in the bay, with the masts of a wrecked ship still thrust above the water. The black inhospitable shores, with the deep groove in the flat of the rock down yonder, which has been worn by the keels of the chiefs' galleys—it all brings back the ancient life of the isles whose records were written in blood by the point of many a sharp sword.

Almost under the shadow of the castle walls, on Rhu Meanish, is the Hill of Pleas, or local judgment seat, where the chief administered the clan laws. It is an oval mound about three feet high with a slight rim round the top. How often I have sat on one of these Justice Mounds in the Highlands and thought of the poor wretches who were led away to the chief's gallows close by !

But the wind is sweeshing through the long grasses, and round the ruined walls, like the sighing of the spirits of the dead who are loth to leave their earthly haunts. The summer world is so wonderful that the white light-house on Scalpay away over by Harris can be clearly seen. The quiet fields behind the castle are beaking in the sun, and over the dazzling Minch the seabirds are crying everlastingly. Peace reigns at Duntulm.

To reach Dunvegan from Duntulm you must travel south again by a road that is to me one long temptation to linger.

At Kilmuir Kirkyard—that wonderful view-point—who does not stop to visit the grave of Flora Macdonald ? From Kilvaxter roadside you look down on the great meadows of Kilmuir where once lay the Loch of Colum-cille which was drained dry in 1824. In this moss you can see quite clearly the site of the old island monastery

of the Columban monks—a tiny church on one islet,
and a larger cashel on another, connected by a causeway. And, if you know where to look, you will also
catch a glimpse of Monkstadt House, to which Flora
Macdonald boldly led Prince Charlie when he was
dressed up as gaukie " Betty Burke." Then the Dun
of Skudiburgh, and from the road above the beautiful
Bay of Uig you look due west across Loch Snizort to
the rocky Ascrib Isles and the Point of Vaternish, and
due south to the line of the purple Coolins.

If lingering were allowed I could tell a tale of all
these places ; and then go sauntering past Earlish with
its little crofts ; Kingsburgh with another salute to
Flora Macdonald ; the great bald kirk of Snizort ; and
so, by Skeabost, Lynedale, Edinbain, and the Fairy
Bridge to Dunvegan. Only—I would be greatly tempted
to travel once more up the road past Stein to Trumpan,
and tell you the tragic story of Lady Grange, who lies
buried in the lonely kirkyard of Trumpan. Nor could
I hold back that other tale of the Battle of the Spoiled
Dykes down yonder by the green flats at the head of
Ardmore Bay.

I have long lost count of the times that I have been
at Dunvegan, and I am saddened now by the thought
that Norman, the twenty-third Chief of Macleod, is
dead.

I came first to Dunvegan in the long ago by sea,
when the distant glimpse of its grey walls seemed the
realisation of a lad's fondest dreams. Since then I
have approached it from every airt, by land and sea,
and of all the great houses I have ever seen, Dunvegan
still holds my heart as the most romantic Hall of Faerie.
It is the only ancient castle in Skye that is to-day
inhabited by a family whose origin is lost in antiquity.

When you cross the doorstep of Dunvegan your one hand is on the balustrade of the present, and your other is groping in the mists of legendry.

The Dunvegan tradition has it that the first Leod of Harris was the son of Olaf the Black, King of Man. Over the front door of Dunvegan there is a stone bearing the arms of the sixteenth chief, and in this coat are the arms of the Isle of Man. Leod was the adopted heir of Paal Baalkeson, who was Sheriff of Skye under the Norse Kings of Man. He owned Sleat, Trotternish, Waternish, and Snizort, and bequeathed all these lands to Leod, passing over his own natural son. Paal was killed in 1231, and with Paal Baalkeson Leod seems to have spent his early days at Duntulm, Dunscaith, and Castle Camus. Some time about 1220 Leod married a daughter of MacCrailt Armuinn, who was Lord of Dunvegan, and owned Duirinish, Bracadale, and Minginish. In the Gaelic MacCrailt became MacArailt, which means the son of Harold, and it is possible that the MacCrailts had been settled at Dunvegan from the end of the ninth century, when many Norsemen were driven away from their native land by Harold Haarfagre. The Armuinns were a kind of second order of nobility and ranked next to the Thanes. This marriage of Leod to MacCrailt's daughter brought Dunvegan and all its wide lands into Leod's family, and to-day Dunvegan is the castle of the twenty-third descendant in unbroken line.

The place was called the Dun of Began, doubtless after one of MacCrailt's ancestors, and there is still a place in Iceland called Becanstadt. Moreover, at Trumpan kirkyard in Vaternish I have seen a tombstone with the name of *RACHEL McRAILD—d.* 1924. So the thirteenth century and the twentieth join hands

at Dunvegan. The atmosphere of this castle in Skye
is a thousand years old, and in the veins of the Chief
who entertained his visitors so courteously there flowed
the blood of MacCrailt Armuinn and the first of all
the Leods.

I cannot here enlarge on the treasures of Dunvegan
which have accumulated in the old keep for centuries.
The Fairy Flag, which was given to Macleod by the
elfin wife he married, as a magic mascot which he
might wave three times in a moment of threatened
danger, and which was indeed waved twice but never
again. The Drinking Horn of Rory Mor, which each
new chief had to drain of liquor to the dregs in one
draught that he might prove his manhood. The
beautiful Dunvegan Cup, which has the date 1493
carved on its rim, and a wooden bowl that is believed
to date from the tenth century, once the property of
Neil Glundubh, who was King of Ulster about 900.
Here also you will see letters from Dr Samuel Johnson
and Sir Walter Scott, both of whom were favoured
guests at Dunvegan. Flora Macdonald's pincushion ;
Prince Charlie's waistcoat and hair ; a portrait of the
wicked chief in black and red ; another of Macleod,
and still another of his lady—both by Sir Henry
Raeburn, and the famous one of Dr Johnson by Sir
Joshua Reynolds. The MacCrimmon bagpipes are
here also, and although I got the offer to put a tune
on them, with a very proper reverence, I declined even
to touch them.

Would that I could tell you some tales of Alastair
Crotach, the eighth chief, and of Sir Rory Mor, the
thirteenth ; of the Fairy Room and its legends ; of the
Sea Gate and the bloody battles ; of the desperate feuds
and burnings between the Macleods and Macdonalds.

Indeed, Skye was a wild world until the 'Forty-Five. I shall never forget passing from the pleasant drawing-room to the dungeon close by, along with the Chief, who lit a candle and let it down on a string through the opening in the stone floor to light the rock-hewn chamber below. From this chamber of horrors there is no possible exit. I can still see the kilted figure standing in the dim light saying with a smile on his face :

" It was down there that my ancestor put his first wife and starved her to death."

We then adjourned to the dining-room and saw the portrait of the Wicked Chief ; one of his first wife whom he got rid of—a rather plain-looking lady ; and another of the second wife—a distinctly good-looking lady. To dine here is to sit cheek by jowl with the tragedies of your own family history.

But my most romantic memory of Dunvegan is a picture of Norman, the twenty-third of his line, standing by the battlements of the ancient tower, in all the dignity of his tartan dress, with the eagle feathers of a chief set gaily in his bonnet. He was gazing into the eye of a June sunset, and at the islands lying in the lap of the sea, and it seemed that he was looking away to Tir-nan-og, that Land of the Ever Young, where war no longer robs the brave of victory, and the happy Celts pursue the arts of peace.

XI

SCUIR NAN GILLEAN

THE PEAK OF THE YOUNG MEN

THE Coolins are the finest mountains in Britain. But be it far from a mere scrambler on the roof of Scotland to speak of rock-climbing in Skye. That is for the experts alone. And yet, if in this magic world of mist and sunshine, islands and seas, one may speak of the hills of heaven, surely the heart and eyes of every mountain lover must instinctively turn to the Coolins !

There is a hardy little army of mountaineers, both old and young, who come year after year to Sligachan, that they may repeat old climbs and conquer new difficulties. For boon companions you will find no better on earth. I do not, however, write for them. Rather am I thinking now of the wayfaring man who comes to Skye for the first time with a natural desire to climb one of these ethereal peaks. Sooner or later he will find himself at Sligachan—that climbers' paradise —and then, all will depend on the weather whether his one precious day is to be a dismal failure or a blessed memory that will live with him to the end of life.

If the day be doubtful, this will happen to him which has happened to most of us. He will probably set out on an excursion up Bruach na Frithe, the easiest summit to reach from Sligachan, but a hill that has a most wonderful view. Not far from the Red Burn the

drizzle will begin. The higher he ascends the burn the heavier the rain will come down. When he crosses the Bealach a' Mhaim, and makes up the slopes of Bruach na Frithe itself, the Skye deluge will be at its best. Yet, when he gains the ridge, the mist may lift for a moment, and right below him in the lower lights he will see the Glen Brittle river gleaming like silver on its way to the sea. But if the rain clouds have settled in, the sooner he retraces his steps the better. He may now be soaked to the skin. He will not need to pick his steps across the Red Burn. He will go right through it without any delicate manœuvres. Even if he sits down on a wet clump of heather to light a pipe, he may do so, for nothing can make him wetter. That is one of the blessings of Skye rain—it does away with a whole host of the politer anxieties.

But Skye is like a sweetheart that is always surprising us with her changing moods. Until you have thus been drenched and disappointed by wet weather among the Coolins, you will never know the bliss of being favoured with a heavenly day for your climb.

I can remember one such day.

We arrived at the Inn in the most brilliant weather. A clear shining day that was all the more wonderful because there had been heavy rain. Not a cloud or shred of mist rested on the splintered peaks, and the visibility was perfect. We were a very jolly company of all ages and sizes. An English climber, his three boys, a tall Scots girl, and her elderly father in a kilt. Old John Mackenzie, who was waiting outside the Inn for the Professor, threw some sage advice at us with a bit of Gaelic humour in the passing. So with a hitch of the rucksack we set off up the old path. Glamaig smiled on us, and we remembered that a fleet-footed

Indian gurkha once reached the top and returned to
the bridge in fifty-five minutes. Little Marsco, which
always looks like a Cardinal with his cap on, gave us
his blessing. The blue Coolins were all about us, and
the long light day was before us.

The route from Sligachan lies south over the moors.
After crossing the Red Burn by the stepping-stones
near the old house, you top a low ridge and see a little
loch lying to your left in Coire Riabhach. Then you
go up a stone shoot into Coire nan Allt Geala. Finally,
the south-east ridge is gained by scrambling up a long
scree. After that you follow the ridge to the right, and
it is now only a matter of time until you reach the
summit. When you are climbing the last hundred feet
or so, hands as well as feet come into play. But for
those who cannot manage the Pinnacles of Scuir nan
Gillean, this is the safe way, which none need despise
who would look upon one of the most glorious views
in the world.

Scrambling up rocks, like those on the top of the
Coolins, entails a certain amount of knee work. So,
when the elderly man in the kilt joined the others on
the summit, youth made some rude remarks about a
pair of ruddy knees.

The view held us spellbound. Here was Skye at
its best. Hot rocks on the high tops. Not a breath of
wind. An almost cloudless sky. The whole of the
western seaboard, the outer Hebrides, the inner isles,
and Eilean a Cheo itself spread out below us like a
map. Looking down into Lota Coire we saw nothing
but desolation. But from Harris to Ross, on sea and
land, it was an elusive world of beauty.

Wherever youth is, age gets little chance to dream
of the sublime, and we were soon brought down to the

ridiculous. For the three boys proceeded to empty their pockets. One had an air pistol and began to shoot at nothing. Another had a whistle which split the silence in two. The third had actually carried up a tiny brass cannon, which he had moulded with his own hands, and a supply of gunpowder. He loaded the cannon twice with powder and shot, and fired at Kyleakin lighthouse—surely a historic moment. For no cannon had ever been fired from the top of Scuir nan Gillean before. Being at a well-known Quaker school in England he was punished for making this weapon of war. There being no loose pebbles on the top, and remembering a well-known rule of mountaineering, that no stone should ever be sent down on those who are below you on a hill, it seemed useless to bring out the catapult.

And it was just as well. For when the mock bombardment was over, we were startled by seeing the face of a young man, who had come up on another climb, looking at us over the edge of the summit rocks. Very hot and dishevelled, he came slowly on to the ledge, followed by another climber. They were members of the English Rucksack Club, and immediately found a fellow-member in the father of the three boys. One of them had sadly torn clothes, both knees of his trousers being ruined, and another part of the same garment almost entirely gone.

"What do you think of these black gabbro rocks? Fine for climbing, are they not?" remarked the man in the kilt, with a smile, as he rubbed some blood from his knees.

"Yes," replied the young Englishman rather slowly, for he was thinking of that part of his garment which he could not see, "one week in the Coolins does more damage than two seasons in Cumberland."

We were just settling in for a talk when once more a head appeared above the rocks from the other side.

" Hullo ! "

And a member of the Junior Scottish Mountain-eering Club thrust his tousled head upon us. A second followed him, and when the rope was taken off the three Scotsmen recognised each other.

So we were a merry party of ten crowded on the top. A feast of coffee and fat things followed. Cameras snapped. Then we separated, and took our own ways down to Sligachan.

The day was done. But the memory of it will linger for ever to cheer many a wintry hour in the far-off city when, amid the rush of ordinary affairs, we lift our eyes above the crowded pavements and behold from the peak of Scuir nan Gillean the islands of the west lying in that azure sea.

Late that night we were fifteen miles from Sligachan. But when we looked to the west the Coolins stood out against the pale green sky like purple mountains in a dream. One crimson cloud still hung above the hills, and the hush of heaven lay over the sea.

XII

THE BRAVE SONS OF SKYE

AN INCOMPARABLE RECORD

THE Celt's love of home has always been pain-drenched by his incurable lust for wandering beyond it. His pride of life is contemptuous of either gold or gear. Gallant beyond all others when he looks into the eyes of death, this has been his battle-cry throughout the ages :

> Danger no refuge holds, and war no peace.

The finest lovers and the fiercest fighters in the world, whose souls have ever been aflame with the high gest, and whose songs are full of the insatiable love which is always tinged with sorrow, through all the adventures of the immemorial years, O Highland hearts, we salute you still !

Far be it from me to set the sons of one Hebrid isle against the sons of another. But it is my privilege now to relate the story of the Brave Sons of Skye, remembering the incomparable record that was compiled over thirty years ago, under that stirring title, by one of themselves, from authentic military sources, with one hundred portraits of those gallant Skyemen.

The Clan system was completely broken down after the 'Forty-Five. But nothing could kill the fighting spirit of the Celt. So, in a remarkably short time

F

after the stramash of Culloden, a wise Government
encouraged the enlistment of thousands of Highlanders
whose fathers had fought for Prince Charlie, and thus
the Highland regiments were raised for service in the
foreign wars.

Here is proof of this wise policy.

William Pitt, afterwards Earl of Chatham, once used
these words in addressing the House of Commons :

" I have sought for merit wherever it could be found.
It is my boast that I was the first Minister who looked
for it, and found it in the mountains of the North.   I
called it forth, and drew into your service a hardy and
intrepid race of men ;   men who, when left by your
jealousy, became a prey to the artifices of your enemies,
and had gone nigh to have overturned the State in the
war before last.   But these men in the last war were
brought to combat on your side ;   they served with
fidelity, as they fought with valour, in every quarter of
the globe."

And what response did the Brave Sons of Skye make
to this appeal of the great Minister of State ?

Only about fifty years after the defeat of the Highlanders at Culloden, and after the shameful treatment
of the fugitives by Cumberland, followed by the Dis-
arming Act of 12th August 1746, which made not only
the carrying of all weapons illegal, but suppressed the
wearing of every kind of Highland dress, the Highlanders began to enlist in the British Army.   We are
told by a former Adjutant-General of the Forces that
in the forty years which preceded the crowning of
Queen Victoria (1797–1837) the Island of Skye alone
provided the armies of Great Britain with 21 lieutenant-
generals and major-generals, 45 lieutenant-colonels, 600
majors, captains and subalterns, 10,000 private soldiers,

120 pipers, 4 governors of British Colonies, 1 Governor-General of India, and 1 adjutant-general of the British Army. More remarkable still, we have it on the same authority that 1600 Skyemen fought in the ranks at Waterloo.

So Skye gave to the Army 666 officers and 10,000 private soldiers, with 120 pipers, within a space of forty years.

It was while Alexander Smith was staying with M'Ian of Ord, that fine old army veteran, that he heard great tales of the Brave Sons of Skye, and so we read in " A Summer in Skye " this remarkable tribute to the men of " An t'Eilean " :

" Love of wandering and pride in military life have been characteristic of all the old families. . . . They have had representatives in every Peninsular and Indian battle-field. . . . Of the miniatures kept in every family more than one-half are soldiers. . . . The tartans waved through the smoke of every British battle, and there were no such desperate bayonet charges as those which rushed to the yell of the bagpipe. At the close of the last and the beginning of the present century, half the farms in Skye were rented by half-pay officers. The Army List was to the island what the Post Office Directory is to London."

What a difference has come over Skye to-day :

O hearts to the hills of old memory true !
In the land of your love there are mourners for you,
As they wander by peopleless lochside and glen,
Where the red deer are feeding o'er homesteads of men.
                                PRINCIPAL SHAIRP.

To write an account of all these Brave Sons of Skye would be an impossible task. So I shall take but one example of a Highland family to show how these remarkable men and women served their King and country at home, and crossed the seas as emigrants to found whole colonies of Gaelic-speaking folks, fighting there when necessary as soldiers of the King, and all the while yearning for the misty island which they could never forget.

There is a remote place on the north-east shores of Trotternish to which my thoughts often fly. It is the historic little estate of Flodigarry. This was one of the seats of the famous family of Macdonald of Kingsburgh, and the tale of Flora Macdonald is one of the romances of the world. Flora married Allan the VIIth of Kingsburgh and Flodigarry, and the story of that family is typical of the Brave Sons of Skye.

Allan's early life was spent at Kingsburgh. His father, Alexander VI of Kingsburgh, was chamberlain to his Chief, and in those days much of the rent was paid in kind—that is, in cattle, sheep, etc. The cattle were collected from every part of the Macdonald estates by drovers, who brought them to Kyle Rhea. There the beasts were taken across the ferry or swam the strait, and were driven all the way south to Falkirk Tryst. Allan, who had all the responsibility for the sale of the cattle, was known locally as " Ailean na mile mart," or " Allan of the Thousand Cattle." About the year 1734 his father, Alexander, bought the estate of Flodigarry from John Martin, and handed over the place to Allan, who took up his residence there.

Allan Macdonald was a handsome man with a powerful physique and a great reputation for wrestling. Early in 1745 Flora Macdonald came back from Edinburgh with Lady Margaret Macdonald to Monkstadt House, the principal seat of the Macdonalds in Skye.

Flodigarry is about six miles across the hills as the crow flies, and Allan must often have crossed the island to cultivate the acquaintance of Flora. But, like all true lovers, they had to wait a long time and pass through much anxiety before they pledged their troth. In June of the same year Flora returned to her father's house at Milton in South Uist.

Then came the stirring events of the 'Forty-Five, the march south to Edinburgh and far-off Derby, the retreat to the Highlands, and the flight of Prince Charlie after Culloden in 1746.

Who can ever forget the story of Prince Charlie and his voyage from Uist to Skye in the boat with Flora Macdonald, who saved him from his pursuers by taking the Prince across the Minch as her female attendant under the name of " Betty Burke " ? The story is too well known to need repetition.

Flora was later taken to London on H.M.S. *Furious* and detained there. No Jacobite ladies were ever brought to trial. They were only " detained " privately in Messengers' Houses—that is, selected prisoners lived in the private premises of Court officials, and their treatment largely depended on the length of their purses. The captivity, however, was not severe, and the Messenger—one Dick—with whom Flora was detained kept in his easy custody many distinguished Jacobites like herself and Æneas Macdonald, the banker. Indeed, Æneas tells us that while in Dick's House he was taken away to Newgate because he was " concerting a jaunt to Windsor with Flora Macdonald."

Flora was not set at liberty till the end of 1747. The reunion of the lovers took place at Monkstadt House, where Sir Alexander and Lady Macdonald gave a ball in honour of Flora's return. Allan's father had also

been confined for the best part of a year in Edinburgh
Castle, and during his absence his estate had been
greatly impoverished. Here is a notice of the wedding
in the *Scots Magazine* : " November 6th, at Armadale,
Sleat, Allan Macdonald, eldest son of Alexander Macdonald of Kingsburgh, married to Miss Flora Macdonald, daughter of Ranald Macdonald of Milton,
deceased. This is the young lady who aided the escape
of the Young Chevalier."

All their children were born at Flodigarry—five sons
and two daughters. Needless to say, the eldest son was
called Charles, after the Prince.

Old Kingsburgh died in 1772, aged 83, and Allan,
after twenty years of happy life at Flodigarry, removed
to Kingsburgh. In July of that year Pennant visited
him, and has recorded that Kingsburgh gave him, on
parting, three gifts—an urn filled with ashes ; a lucky
Druidical glass bead, with serpents marked on it ; and
a Roman coin, a *Denarius* of the Emperor Trajan, which
was found near Loch Greshornish. Pennant suggests
that it may have been picked up by an island soldier
when skirmishing with the Romans farther south.

In the autumn of 1773 Samuel Johnson and Boswell
paid Kingsburgh a visit, and Boswell has left us an
inimitable picture of Allan Macdonald :

" Kingsburgh was completely the picture of a gallant
Highlander. . . . He had his tartan plaid thrown about
him, a large blue bonnet with a knot of blue riband like
a cockade, a brown short coat of a kind of duffel, a tartan
waistcoat with gold buttons and gold button-holes, a
bluish philibeg and tartan hose. He had jet black hair
tied behind, and was a large, stately man, with a steady,
sensible countenance."

Of Kingsburgh's Lady, Johnson writes these words,

which are now carved on Flora Macdonald's monument at Kilmuir : " Flora Macdonald, a name that will be mentioned in history, and if courage and fidelity be virtues, mentioned with honour."

Both Johnson and Boswell slept in the Prince's room at Kingsburgh, and Johnson occupied the bed which the Prince had slept in. They talked that night of the unique experience, and in the morning Boswell found on the bedroom table a slip of paper on which Johnson had written these words :

> Quantum cedat virtutibus aurum.
> (With virtue weighed, what trash is gold !)

Doubtless Johnson was thinking of the utter loyalty of the Highlanders to their Prince, for not one of them was tempted by the £30,000 reward which the Government offered for news of his whereabouts.

But Boswell remarks that Kingsburgh was embarrassed in his affairs and was even then thinking of emigration. So the next year, in August 1774, Allan Macdonald and Flora, his wife, with all their family, except Charles and John, sailed in the ship *Baliol* from Campbeltown to Wilmington, on the Cape Fear River, in North Carolina.

What an adventure emigration was in those days ! The *Baliol* was attacked by a French privateer, and a fierce fight took place. Flora Macdonald refused to go below when the firing began, but remained on deck where all her family were engaged in battle. During the mêlée her arm was broken, and a young clansman, Kenneth Macdonald, who had studied surgery in Glasgow, set her arm and bound it up.

Their fellow-countrymen gave the Macdonalds a great welcome to Carolina, where Flora's fame had

preceded her.   At Cross Creek, a hundred miles
further up the river, there was a Highland settlement.
But they moved on to Cameron's Hill, and, finally,
Allan bought land in an outlying part of the colony,
and called his new home Killiegray.

The Highlanders arrived just about the time the
Home Government and the American colonists were
beginning to quarrel, and in 1775 the crisis came.
After a skirmish at Lexington in April the Battle of
Bunker Hill was fought on 17th June.   So in Carolina,
as long before in Skye, the Celts heard the old call
to arms :

> Danger no refuge holds, and war no peace.

A regiment of Highland emigrants was at once
raised, and the whole corps was dressed and accoutred
in the manner of the Black Watch, under the name of
the Royal Highland Emigrants.   Allan Macdonald
became a Captain, and his son Alexander was appointed
a Lieutenant.   Then followed fierce fighting and years
of service.   Both were taken prisoners, but were released
on exchange.   They saw service at New York, Halifax,
the Spanish River, Cape Breton, and cruising about the
Canadian coast.   Then they remained in Nova Scotia
until peace was declared in 1783, when Allan and the
other Captains of the 2nd Battalion received from the
Government a grant of 5000 acres of land near Halifax.

But the old yearning for home overcame Flora and
her daughters, and long before the war was over they
returned to Skye, in the year 1779.   Allan saw the
fighting through, and then, like many another Highland
gentleman, he trekked home in 1784 to take up the old
holding at Kingsburgh.   For six happy years he and
his wife lived there, until Flora died in 1790.   Allan

lingered till 1792, when he also passed over. Such is the story of an illustrious Highland family.

To-day Allan and Flora lie side by side in the old Kirkyard of Kilmuir. I saw a new-made grave close by, and farther off I took a drawing of an old grey effigy of a knight in armour. For love is old yet ever new, and the sob at the heart is the same in all generations. The summer day seemed almost hurting in its beauty as I sat among the graves and dreamed. Flora's Monument towered above the humbler headstones, and looked right out to the Hebrid Isles, which lay on the rim of the west like islands of the blest on a sea of glass.

> For the stillness they feel o'er the wilderness spread
> Is not Nature's own silence, but that of the dead ;
> E'en the lone piping plover and small corrie burn
> Seem sighing for those that will never return.
>
> PRINCIPAL SHAIRP.

XIII

PABBAY

THE ISLAND OF THE PRIEST

IT is no small mercy to remember a day of great beauty
and pass on the vision to those who have never lived
through its hours. To recreate such a day is to make
the world flash with wonder for those who cannot see
for themselves.

In this throng world we cannot be always tramping
the pleasant roads or sailing the summer seas. But at
least in wintry days or in hours of harassment we can
always see with

> That inward eye
> Which is the bliss of solitude.

So can I see at this moment a little island of the
West which always reminds me of that classic isle of
Revelation called Patmos, where John the Dreamer was
exiled long ago. Like the mystic island in the Ægean,
Pabbay, or *Pap-ey*, which is the Norseman's name for
the Priest's Isle, lies so near and yet so far from the
greater isles and the mainland townships that the holy
man who lived there in ancient times must often have
felt doubly imprisoned because his eyes could daily
look across the narrow seas to more populous shores
than his own. To-day, but for a crofting clachan here
and there, the shores of the Hebrid Isles are lonely and

silent. But when the priest of Pabbay set up his cell, the Western Isles were peopled by Celts and Norsemen who for centuries waged terrific war on one another. To them the Gospel of Peace was carried by many a heroic monk.

Pabbay lies between the wild Coolins of Skye and the mountains of Applecross. Although it is but a flat circle of sheep-grass, yet it floats amid a panorama that is full of wonders, when the morning sunlight turns the waters into a sea of glass, or the summer sun dies in splendour behind the hills of Skye and steeps the Western world in a mist of gold. To gaze across the twilight seas to this little Island of the Priest when the clouds of evening, all golden rimmed, are floating like islands of the blessed in the liquid sky, is to be conscious of a beauty that is almost pain. So day by day that little island drew my desires, and I longed for the time when I would be able to go over and surprise its secrets for myself.

The day came. The sea was sparkling and the skies were blue from rim to rim, with a little cloud of pure white incense rising from the top of Scuir nan Gillean. The mountains of Applecross, blue-grey and ethereal, rose above the desolate shores of Loch Kishorn. The white boat raced through the tumbling tides and made for the Kyle of Scalpay. We watched a school of porpoises playing near Strollamus, where the river falls quietly into the narrows after its brawling journey from the screes of Ben-na-Cailleach. Then, back to Pabbay, with its rocky reefs and little pier.

The shores are mostly shingle and tilted rocks. The black wrack-strewn skerries reach out long treacherous fingers into the shallow seas as if to catch the unwary when the tides are running and the merry men are roaring with laughter in the storm. Long ago the whole island was covered with forest. Now it is one bare flat sheep-walk with two tiny strips of wood planted in the very centre. A solitary house, two hundred sheep, a few horses, and sea birds that are for ever complaining round the shores—that is the beginning and the end of life on Pabbay. But in olden times the island was infested with pirates and robbers—" neyre ane myle in lenthe, full of woodis, guid for fishing, and a main shelter for thieves and cut-throats." A fine gathering-ground for all who were outlaws, with its skerries, its dark woods, and its famous fishing-ground.

The fine fishing remains to this day. Has not Lord Knutsford written recently of a great catch he once had on the fishing bank off Pabbay ? But you must anchor your boat off Pabbay by the middle of Longay Island ; mark in front of you Dun Caan, the highest peak in Raasay ; and behind you the straits of the Kyle of Loch Alsh. His catch in four hours amounted to 353 gurnard ; 10 cod—four of which weighed 20 lbs., 18 lbs., and two of 17 lbs. ; 30 haddocks and various other fish. This fishing bank still yields splendid sport.

To those wild men of Pabbay long ago came a priest. He built his cell and chapel beside the one tiny stream-let on the island, and in the course of the generations a graveyard was added close by. To-day you can trace that ancient settlement by a rickle of grey stones. On this very spot a succession of holy men preached Christ to the robbers. The lonely monk would often look across to Rhu Ardnish in Skye, where by a little creek stood Kil Ashik, or *cill-aiseag*, the Church of the Ferry. The strait is but a mile across. The Skye folks still bury in Kil Ashik, and there by the site of the old Celtic Church you will find the remains of a finely built holy

well. How often must Saint Maolrubha himself have
been ferried across to Pabbay and to Kil Ashik from
his own beloved Applecross ! Indeed the Western Isles
are steeped in the atmosphere of dead saints.

We spent the livelong day basking in the sunshine.
The blue reek rose from the fire among the rocks, for
we loitered through the hours. The cool green waters
were buoyant and delicious to bathe in. The distant
corn patches of the crofts at Breakish gleamed golden
in the September sun. The fine old road across the
island is laid with the closest of sea turf. The highest
point of Pabbay is only 89 feet above the sea, but little
cliffs rise along the southern shores beyond the Bay of
the Chapel. On such a summer day, the dim blue hills,
the green-shored islands and the limitless plain of sparkling sea make the Western world a very dream of heaven.
There was peace on Pabbay that day—peace and beauty,
with a sough of old-time history in the warm winds, and
a hint of lost things in the cry of the wild birds as they
flashed white wings above the sea.

But there is much to see and more to find on this
Priest's Island. For early in the nineteenth century
there came a searcher after truth, across the seas with
a hammer in his hand. We traced his steps along the
shore and up and down the little cliffs, seeking for what
Hugh Miller made known to the whole world—the
wealth of fossils on the Pabbay shore. He explored the
island, ransacked its rocks and beaches, and examined
the nodules in its little cliffs. Then he declared that
this green island was so rich in geological specimens
that despite its limited area the fossils of Pabbay would
fill a museum.

" They rise in thousands and tens of thousands on
exposed plains of the sea-washed strata, standing out

in bold relief like sculpturings on ancient tombstones,
at once mummies and monuments—the dead and
carved memorials of the dead . . . every rolled pebble
is a casket with old pictorial records locked up
within."

Here again was a man of Revelations laying bare
the history of the earth on this same Robbers' Isle.
Many years ago a friend gave me a handful of fossils
from Pabbay's Isle—*Gryphæa incurva*—and through all
these intervening years I have desired with a great
longing to hunt the dead along this very shore.

Now I am wandering at will, searching the beaches
and losing all sense of time among the wonders of an
ageless world. But, since the Man with the Hammer
wrote " The Testimony of the Rocks," countless visitors
have robbed Pabbay of its fossil fortune, and Hugh
Miller's words seem strangely large to-day.

One find, however, that sunny day was full of co-
incidence and chance. The shepherd gave me a beautiful
ammonite which had lain for long on the window-sill of
his porch. The fossil was embedded in a large flat water-
rolled pebble which had been picked up at some time or
other round the shores. When I got back to the little
company round the fire, I found that another had been
searching the shores and had found among the myriad
pebbles the thin top of a flat stone on which were
impressed the markings of an ammonite. I placed the
one on the other. They fitted to perfection. Each
of us had happened on the other half of the same
fossil.

The Monk in his Cell and the Man with the Hammer
—between them they have made Pabbay for ever an
Island of Revelations. The one with his simple
news of Christ in an age of grave deeds and pagan

superstitions ; the other with his newer light of knowledge which has shed fresh wonder on the creation of the world.

So, when the sun began to wester, and the evening breeze was making the merry men dance about the skerries, the white boat bore us back to Haco's Kyle, and we landed once more on the Doorstep of Skye, with memories in our hearts that will never fade.

ROSS

XIV

THE SEA GATES OF WESTER ROSS

I.—BRAEMORE, BROOM, AND DUNDONELL

BETTER to travel alone than to travel in ill company. But when I set out from Beauly that June morning, the company was as good as the weather. The sky was one swirl of blue and white. All the world was dressed in green. The birds were singing in every wood. The yellow broom blazed along the roadsides like tongues of golden flame. When your fellow travellers are like yon company you never trouble about milestones, and each day, like a fine tune fingered by a skilly player, comes to an end all too soon. A June morning in Strathconon would send the heart of a pessimist leaping. So, we passed through Muir of Ord and Urray, crossed the Orrin, and made for Moy Bridge, above which the waters of the Conon and the Blackwater meet. A fine heartsome country this—flat farm lands, green fields, leafy woods, and flashing rivers all the way from Beauly to Contin. But, we were making for wilder parts than these, and our eyes were continually on the dim blue mountains of Wester Ross, which you can see so well from the open flats about the Beauly Firth.

At the Falls of Rogie we sat on the rocks and

sweltered in the sun. But the roar of the water as it came tumbling below the precarious swing bridge was not loud enough to drown the skirl of the pipes or the peals of laughter. The years began to slip off us, like rusty garments. June had captured our souls. The brothers of the road were young again.

> Oh, hear me sing—If youth but knew
>   The glory of his April day,
>   Would he not cast the year away
> For one more dawn of dream and dew ?
>
> For what shall unto age accrue
>   If youth from joyance turn and stray ?
>   Autumn is but the Spring grown grey,
> It's harvest roses mixed with rue. . . .
>
> If youth but knew—if youth but knew !

But we were far as yet from the sound of the western sea. The road to the golden gates of Wester Ross begins at Garve and ends at Achnasheen. Go up the one and come down the other, and you will complete the magic circle of those sunset lochs which make the glory of Ross-shire. Take as many days or weeks as you please, but this at least is what you will see.

Having left the beauties of Loch Achilty and Contin behind you, the road sweeps along the side of Loch Garve, and then turns sharply to the right. Here is the beginning of that desolate highway which will at last bring you to the shores of the glamorous West from which you can look straight into the eyes of the setting sun. The long straight moorland road keeps ascending by the side of the Glascarnoch river for fifteen miles from Garve to the little Loch Droma,

G

which, as its name tells you, lies on the very ridge of
the hill.   The old road is called the Dirrie More—
only in Gaelic the word sounds more like " Cherry-
Vore," and means the " great oak forest."   These wastes
were once covered with timber.   But the old place-name
has outlasted the trees, and the Dirrie More always
reminds me of that other Dirrie Beg of St Columba in
the north of Ireland, for which he sighed when he pushed
off in his coracle from the shores of Erin with the dool
of farewell in his soul :—

> My Derry, my little oak grove,
> My dwelling, and my little cell !

Others have translated Dirrie More as the " great
ascent," which it also is.   But, one way or another,
doire or *direadh*, it is a stey brae yet, and you can see
the roots of the old forest trees still sticking through
the peat bogs.

Then comes the great surprise.   From Loch Droma
the road descends, and you plunge from the wilderness
into a paradise of woods and wild flowers, through the
Braemore Forest, to the shores of Loch Broom.   It was
a famous engineer who, with the aid of a wonderful
climate, made this wilderness blossom like the rose.
So, after the long dreary ascent of the Dirrie More
come these dense woods in the gorge of the Droma
river.   The lordly house of Braemore stands high above
the woods.   The rhododendrons splash the roadside
with colour.   Not only the old-fashioned purple of the
ponticum, but blazing reds intermingled with delicate
pinks and pure whites.   For we are now nearing the
milder regions of the sea gates of Wester Ross, where
flowers grow in a prodigal luxuriance and the balmy
winds of the West blow softly on the face.

It's a warm wind, the west wind, full of bird's cries ;
I never hear the west wind but tears are in my eyes.
For it comes from the west lands, the old brown hills
And April's in the west wind, and daffodils.

It's the white road westwards is the road I must tread
To the green grass, the cool grass, and rest for heart and head,
To the violets and the warm hearts and the thrushes' song,
In the fine land, the west land, the land where I belong.

JOHN MASEFIELD.

But the wonder of Braemore to me will always be
the gorge of Corriehalloch and the Falls of Measach.
A little path on the left leads down from the road,
through the trees, to a suspension bridge. As you stand
on the bridge you are looking down into what must
surely be the finest gorge in Scotland. This narrow
gorge has been cut clean through the rocks by the age-
long action of the river. The flat perpendicular walls
are covered with a wealth of ferns and mosses. The
glorious vista holds you like a spell. I do not know
the exact depth of this ravine. But if anyone will gather
a few pieces of wood, drop each one from the centre of
the bridge, and watch the stick falling, falling, and still
falling, until it strikes the black water far below, he will
very soon be conscious of the height on which he is
standing. If he is not a lover of the beetling crags, he
may then perhaps become conscious of an intolerable
sensation at the pit of the stomach, which will very soon
make him leave the bridge. One man's pleasure in this
heady world is very often another man's pain.

For the next seven miles you travel down the wooded
side of Strathmore, until you come to the seawrack at
Inverlael. As at Braemore, so at Inverbroom, the
flowers of June will greet you with a smile. Yonder,
across the valley, stand the church and manse of Loch

Broom. Then the road rises, and the winds are laden
with the salt tang of the sea. At Leckmeln you will
exclaim again at the rhododendrons, and be conscious
that the soft peace of the west country is sliding into
your soul. A mile or two more, and you catch a gleam
of white houses on a long point, a little harbour, a few
trees, an old church, a cosy inn behind the trees, a swirl
of reek rising into the air—and you are at Ullapool,
just in time to see the sun going down beyond the
Summer Isles.

Ullapool is a quaint, overgrown village, which was
set down on this promontory by those who knew the
ways of herring-fleets. In 1823 a large ship put into
Ullapool and was destroyed by fire. Her cargo was
partially saved, and among the salvage were several
casks of fish hooks. These were the first factory hooks
known in the district, and ever since the life of Ullapool
has depended on the fishing industry. But, hooks,
herrings or haddocks, here is a world all its lone at the
back of beyond, basking in the sunshine by the shores
of Loch Broom. I can see Ullapool in my mind's eye
yet, although I am far from the smell of the sea to-day.
The little fence which goes down to the shore beyond
the village, the long spit of land running out into the
water beyond the river mouth, the crofting townships
straggling along the hillside with their little windows
twinkling in the sun ; and, far out, at the mouth of the
loch, on the rim of the shining sea, a blue island, like
the faintest cloud, where Achiltiebuie looks across the
Bay of Badentarbet to the Summer Isles.

Those who would find the nearest way to Dundonnell Inn have only to row across the narrow loch
to Altnaharrie, and a five-mile walk on the old road
across the hills will bring them down to Dundonnell

STRATH NA SHEALLAG, DUNDONNELL

Lodge at the head of Little Loch Broom. The road rises about seven hundred feet in the first mile, and from the summit of the hilll there is a magnificent view of the Teallach Mountains.

But the long way round is generally the best for him who would see the world, and those who retrace their steps from Ullapool to Braemore will never grudge a single mile of that glorious road.

The road to Dundonnell branches off from the Dirrie More road to the right, a little way above the Falls of Measach, crosses the Droma, runs down the other side of the gorge for a mile, then strikes to the left up Glenmore towards Loch a Bhraoin, and so by Fain right through the Dundonnell Forest down to Little Loch Broom. Just before Fain it touches one thousand feet, and all the way you are gazing at the great Teallach Mountains. Here is a paradise for the mountaineer, but even those who travel by the road will find among the hills of Dundonnell a sanctuary of heavenly peace.

The road by which we are now travelling has always been called the Destitution Road. That name dates from the time it was made—somewhere about the year 1851—after the great potato famine. There was so much distress in the Highlands at that time that Government aid was called in, and a regular Destitution Committee was formed to advance money for the relief of the people. The potato famine began in 1846, and for a long time after that, roads were made in this part of the Highlands to provide work for the poverty-stricken crofters. The Destitution Committee agreed to advance several thousands of pounds for this purpose ; the local road trustees and proprietors, like Mackenzie of Gairloch and Mackenzie of Dundonnell, advanced similar sums, and so the Dundonnell, the Poolewe, the Aultbea, and the Gairloch roads, together with those on the west side of Loch Ewe, were all either made or set out in this time of distress.

It is an old story now. But, as we sit and rest by the side of the stream under a great wall of cliffs before descending into the lower tree-clad glen, it is good to remember that in those old days some of the Highland proprietors almost ruined themselves in their anxiety to help their starving people. For they loved the lands they owned, they knew personally the people who lived on them, and the blood of the old chiefs was flowing in their veins.

As we pass down the green strath the quaint, white-washed, three-storey house of Dundonnell reminds us of these austere times. It is an unspoiled example of the bald Scots mansion, a more modern lodge standing lower down the valley across the stream. You can now see the hill road from Altnaharrie dropping down the brae face behind the lodge into the lonesome world of Strathbeg. The Inn of Dundonnell stands on the road-side at the head of the loch, which has, like all the sea-lochs of Ross, its own outgait to the Minch, with a slant to the west, as if for ever seeking the setting sun. There is nothing dramatic about the scenery of Little Loch Broom. Crofting clachans are dotted here and there along the shores—Badrallach, Rhireavach, Scoraig on the north shore ; Badcaul, Durnamuck, Badluchrach on the south—isolated little communities, with a whiff of peat reek at every door, their patchwork of hayfields and cornlands making a fringe of green-and-yellow tartan above the restless sea.

In these crofting townships lies the real life of the Highlands to-day. Winds from the west, driving rain and creeping mist. Sunbursts that make the wild wet world shine with a celestial beauty. The sound of the sea breaking on the shore, and the smell of the red wrack in every wind that blows. Pearly days in summer, when the floating clouds and the dim blue islands mingle their mysteries on the rim of the ocean. A whiff of honey from the purple heather and sun burning the cheeks like fire. Dark nights of winter, when stars quiver above the inky hills, and the restless sea-birds keep wailing on the edge of the racing tides ! Blessing be on you, oh children of the West, as you hold your *ceilidh* round the fire. For in winter storm or summer sun, in the crofts of home or in the furthest lands of the world, yours are the hearts that can never forget.

To-day a wind from the West out over the hills came blowing—
   Ah, how it made dim dreams and memories start !
And I thought that I smelt in my room the wild thyme growing
   And the scent of the sweet bogmyrtle filled my heart.

Go back, O breath of the hills ! Would that we went together !
   Tell how their lost child fares.
Whisper among the bracken, and say to the broom and the heather
   That still my heart is theirs.

Steal quietly as a dream along the glens that we know,
   The glens that shall fade from me only when I lie dying ;
Sink into peace in the quiet places, silent and low,
   Where the dust men know not is " lying."

LAUCHLAN MACLEAN WATT.

XV

THE SEA GATES OF WESTER ROSS

II.—GRUINARD, EWE, AND GAIRLOCH

HEAVEN is kind to some of us when we take the road, for it was a perfect summer day when we left Dundonnell for Gruinard, Ewe, and Gairloch. Only those who know that region can imagine what it is like on such a day. These are the sea gates of Wester Ross— the two Loch Brooms, Gruinard Bay, Loch Ewe, and Gairloch—five arms of the sea which have wormed themselves into the land. The great mountains of Fisherfield, Gruinard, Dundonnell, Braemore, and Inverlael forests tower behind them. Low-lying hills and green flats sweep round their shores. Islands lie in the lap of their sheltered waters. All of them look right across the waters of the Minch to the north-west. The views seaward to the blue hills of Skye and the far-off Isle of Lewis draw the eye with a strange wistfulness. Perhaps it is that you are always airting your soul to the *Tir-nan-og* which lies out yonder in the golden mists of sunset. Perhaps it is that here is a land of infinite variety—wild mountains, inland lochs of great beauty, seaboards that are as green as an emerald, with a climate that will grow tropical plants. Endless townships of crofting communities lie far away from the busy haunts of men. The beauty of these sunset sea-lochs gives you the sense of ever looking towards infinity.

Gruinard, Ewe, and Gairloch—strange is it not that each of these lochs holds in its arms one solitary island which snuggles between the headlands—the Isle of Gruinard, the Isle of Ewe, and the Isle of Longay. And Rhu Rhe—how often in the days, which are old now, have we steered for that landfall when the white wings were all spread to catch the favouring breeze, and we raced northwards over the sea !

The road from Dundonnell Inn to Gruinard skirts the shore of Little Loch Broom, and then slants to the left across the open moors. The hills on this promontory are low, the road never rises more than 530 feet, and it is only five miles from the shore of the one loch to the shore of the other. But from the top the view to the west opens out in a quiet beauty.

The whole circle of Gruinard Bay now lies before you, with the Isle of Gruinard but a mile from the shore, the Priests' Isle five miles farther out, and all the Summer Isles beyond. On a clear day you can see the Long Island lying on the rim of the Minch like a blue cloud. The loch is green-shored and almost treeless, except round Gruinard House and at the head of the bay, where there is a little wood. White and bald and lonely by the sea stands this pleasant house, with green machars all about it, far from the busy world, and beautiful for situation. White sands gleam at the head of the loch. The waters of Gruinard, like the waters of all sea-lochs where there is sand, are deliciously iridescent, with blues and greens and purples, when the sun shines. To swim in such waters and to tread such sandy sea floors is like sporting in the glittering seas of heaven.

Then from Little Gruinard you climb steadily up the steep test road, which is really cut out of the face

of the cliff. The gradient is one in seven, and there is
no relief for the collar work as you pech up the steep
incline with a bundle on your back or creep up it in a
car. Leaning over the retaining wall at the top of this
precipitous road, you can catapult a stone right into the
sea far below. Yonder gleam the yellow sands, where
the fairies have dyed the waters green and blue. A
great bluff of the cliff on the left hides the prospect of
the islands. But the bare headlands recede one after
the other, into the summer haze, and the mountains
rise beyond them in a series of dim blue tops.

The villages of Gruinard are quaintly named. First
Coast, Second Coast, Sand, Laid, Idrigil, Mellon Idrigil,
and Mellon Charles. But the Gaelic name of First Coast
is *Bad an t'sluig*, or the Cluster in the Gullet; and the
Gaelic name of Second Coast is *An t'oirthir donn*, or the
Brown Front. And yet, who that passes through them
to-day ever realises how much may be in a name, or
questions why the one is called a *Cluster* and the other
a *Front* !

But these villages have many of their little houses
huddled together in a close cluster, because here in old
days, and indeed until comparatively modern times,
these cottars cultivated their land on the old system of
" run-rig." Each little field was divided into separate
ridges or " rigs " which ran parallel, and were cultivated
by different tenants. One tiny field might be divided
among four or eight people, so their cottages or black
houses had to be clustered closely together. Naturally
such a clachan would be full of jealousies, for each man
made his own " rig " as high as possible so that none
of the soil would be carried to his neighbour's ground.
Only the crown of the ridge was ploughed, and the
intervening unploughed spaces, or " baulks," were

choked with briers, nettles, stones, and water. In ancient times, when the cottars cast out, as they often did, one would set fire to another's standing corn. Thus it was necessary to divide or " *baulk* " their little " run-rigs " by these strips of unploughed land. This vicious system was a serious obstacle to any progress in agriculture. Hence the old Scots proverb : " Mak' nae baulks o' guid bere land." So much for First Coast and the meaning of its cluster of houses.

But what of Second Coast and its Front ? The houses nearly all look eastward, and the word Front means East. For, in old times the Celt always named the airts, or points of the compass, from the position of a man facing the rising sun. So, Front meant East, Left meant North, Right meant South, and Back meant West. How much ancient lore may lie behind the name of a village—a clustered clachan on the hill, or a row of white-washed houses fronting the rising sun !

As I grow older I travel slower—not because my legs are failing me—but because there is so much to learn and see and hear in the most outlandish spot on this most wonderful world. For the curse of this age is hurry, and hurry leaves no time to find out anything. Therefore, for knowledge of the oddities of human nature and out-of-the-way places, how much better are the legs of a man than the gears of a car ! The Priest's Island out yonder in the blue sea reminds you of those lonely hermits of Christ who lived in caves and raised the torch of truth in a dark land. The very name of Idrigil gives you visions of Norse Vikings and brave sea-jarls. Here at Sand of Idrigil, a little ruined chapel reminds you of the Columban settlement that was consecrated on this spot by some faithful Ionic monk long long ago.

It was at Mellon Idrigil that a strange sight was seen one Sacrament Sunday in 1822. The whole sea between the Priest's Isle and Cailleach Head was full of ships of war. From the ships a vast number of soldiers in scarlet coats were rowed ashore in boats which landed them on the rocks at Mellon Idrigil. One old cailleach, when she saw the soldiers, ran and buried all her valuables in a box beneath the sand. The girls in the shielings of Rhu Mor took to their heels and hid among the low hills for fear of the redcoats. Then, in a moment, the soldiers were no more, and the great ships vanished like a mist before the eyes. Yet, the old cailleach's box of trinkets was hidden in the sand ; and the girls, all silent with wonder, came slowly back from the hills. Strange is this gift of sight in the mystic North, and vision in a Celt is strong. A hundred years after, these very sea-lochs were full of British warships and sailormen during the Great War.

While we are still resolving our doubts and thinking of this freit of phantom ships and soldiers, we are over the hill and down at Aultbea, with the Green Isle of Ewe lying like an emerald gleaming in the summer sea.

For miles the road skirts the side of Loch Ewe, past Drumchork, and Loch Tournaig to Poolewe. At Tournaig a charming house stands by the side of the little freshwater Loch na Daline. Here you will find a fairy garden of fruits and flowers growing luxuriantly in what must originally have been a stone quarry or a pit among the heather. The road dives inland for a few miles, and finally emerges at the head of Lochewe, a little way from Inverewe House.

A kirk, a clachan, and an old kirkyard, a bridge, a river with a salmon pool below, an inn to rest in, and the sea for an outgate—surely Poolewe is one of the

THE KING'S HIGHWAY, GRUINARD

most enchanting spots in Wester Ross! The climate is almost tropical in summer and the winters are moist and mild. Across the bay, on the shore of the sheltering arm of Ploc-ard, stands Inverewe House, which was built in 1865 by Mr Osgood MacKenzie, the author of that interesting book, "A Hundred Years in the Highlands." Here he planted trees and laid out a garden by the shore in the form of a terraced amphitheatre, and soon under his loving hands the wilderness began to blossom like the rose. Masses of brilliant flowers and the most delicious fruits, rare semi-tropical creepers, with myrtles and roses everywhere, made an earthly paradise of this bare promontory. The warm moist climate seemed to intensify the very colour of the flowers, and the garden became a blaze of brilliance. Here you may walk by the waters of a Highland loch, and yet enjoy the beauties of a garden which might be on the shores of Bellagio, while up yonder in the wilds of Aridh Charr you can stalk stags or shoot ptarmigan in snow and storm. But, alas—during the Great War the pleasant house of Inverewe was partly destroyed by fire. The story goes that when all seemed lost a ship of war sent a shot right through the blazing wing and so saved from further destruction the part which is still standing. Green flats by the shore; the little clachan across the water, with the great hills behind; soft winds laden with the scent of flowers in summer, and the salt tang of the sea when the wild wet winters come—here, tucked in behind his wooded promontory, and with his windows always winking to the southern sun, a great old Highlander touched his territory with a loving hand, and created a paradise in the lonely North.

The road to Gairloch crosses the bridge, goes up the riverside and over the moors to the right by Loch

Tollie. Every mile of a Highland road, no matter how lonely, has its own interest, if only you have the knowledge of its past. Yonder is a little island near the shore of Loch Tollie. Long ago human hands fashioned it and built upon it a crannog which was used in later times as a fortress by the Macbeaths and Macleods. Farther on, at *Blar na Fala*—the Plain of Blood—the cattle used to be gathered for blood-letting. Until 1772, according to Pennant, and as late as the beginning of the nineteenth century, according to local tradition, this practice of drawing blood as an article of food from cattle was common in the Highlands. Beyond that still, on the right-hand side of the road, you will see a funeral cairn to mark the place where the bearers rested the coffin and added a stone to the cairn. Then on the left-hand of the road, nearer Gairloch, there is a large boulder called *Clach nam Brog*, which means the Shoe Stone. For here the women who had walked thus far over the hills to church barefooted, usually sat down to put on their shoes and stockings. From the Achter-cairn brae there is a glorious prospect to the west, across the Bay of Gairloch to the heavenly hills of Skye. So, we descend to the last of the sea gates of Wester Ross, which lies looking right into the eye of the sunset.

To some people Gairloch means a great hotel. But to me it will always mean lying at anchor in Flowerdale Bay with the beauties of June all about me, and the old *Tigh Dige*, or family house of the Mackenzies of Gairloch standing in the sun among the trees, its little outside stair all buried in greenery. Lying on the warm white deck, looking over the gunwale, these crystalline waters of the West are so clear that the stones on the bottom far below were distinctly seen.

It was the time of the summer Sacrament in the year 1895. Fishing boats sailed into the bay, full of black-robed men and women, who had come from far to attend the great Feast of Remembrance. That very day, I well remember, we had walked through Kerrysdale to Loch Maree and back again. On the roads as on the sea, hundreds of people were gathering at the *Leabaidh na Bo Baine*—the Bed of the White Cow—a green paradise which Fingal is said to have hollowed out, that his white cow might bring forth her calves in peace. Round the sides of this grassy amphitheatre two thousand people could with ease be seated. Old men and women, fishermen and their wives, shepherds from the sheepfolds and ghillies from the hill—they were all making for the green hollow to keep their tryst with God. Then—a sound of Gaelic lilting and the singing of a psalm, slow and solemn and sweet to the ears of those who understand.

That night the sun went down in great glory over the summer sea. But the night was short-lived. For dawn came up so swiftly on the back of dusk that, as it rose, mysterious, behind the inky hills, it kissed the lambent afterglow. Somewhere, hidden among the trees on the ghostly shore, lay the green hollow, silent and empty now—and yet!—sacramental still with the memory of a plaintive psalm and the Presence which greeted the fishermen of Galilee in the light of an Eastern dawn.

XVI

A DREAM OF ISLE MAREE

SOUNDS OF THE SUMMER NIGHT

IT seems like a dream, as I think of it on this dark December day. The summer night all luminous with the afterglow of sunset. The waters of Maree like a sea of glass mingled with fire. The big boat making for the islands. The piper at the bow, flinging weird blasts across the waters, his ear leaning fondly to the drones, as if to catch the gallantries and sobs of the dead generations whose dust now lies in the graves of the little isle. A group of men sat silently in the stern, and the great hills—Slioch and his brother bens— listened as they must have done from the first of time to the sound of battle cries or love lilts rising from the loch shores far below.

We had come that day through Kerrysdale, a boon brotherhood if ever there was one. Now—a strange quietness fell upon us as the keel of the boat grated on the shore of the burial Isle of St Maelrubha. It was twilight among the trees, and we stepped softly through them to the place of graves. There, in a little clearing of the wood, we found what we had come to see—the stones of the Dead Lovers, the site of the Hermit's Cell, the Well of Magic Waters, and the Dead Tree with countless coins hammered into its leaning trunk as offerings to the spirit of the well.

Here, indeed, is a place of ancient sacrifice. In the dim long ago, which no history book ever describes, when our land was wholly pagan, there doubtless stood here an altar of sacrifice. Then came Columba and his apostolic monks, planting the cross on these old worship sites. A hundred years after that came Maelrubha, the apostle of Christ, to Applecross. He found the altar stone on this very isle, and built his hermitage with a little chapel alongside. From that day to this there have been Christian graves on Isle Maree, and the sacred holly still grows on the island.

Here, from time immemorial, Druids or priests offered bulls in sacrifice to their god. St Maelrubha may have permitted this ancient rite to continue—for, strange to say, in this very district the sacrifice of bulls continued until after the Reformation !

There is a minute of the Presbytery of Lochcarron dated " At Appelcross, 5th September 1656—*inter alia* . . . the minister being inquired of his brethren, of the many enormities of the parochin of Lochcarrone and Appilcross, declaires some of his parochinirs to be superstitious especiallie in sacrificeing at certaine tymes at the Loch of Mourie, especiallie the men of Auchaseallach. . . . The said day the Presbyterie of Dingwall . . . haveing mett at Appilcross and findeing amongst uther abhominable and heathenishe practices that the people in that place were accustomed to sacrifice bulls at a certaine tyme, uppon the 25 of August, which day is dedicate, as they conceive, to Sn. Mourie as they call him."

Another minute of date, " At Kenlochewe, 9 Septr. 1656," refers to " the abhominationes within the parochin of Gairloch in sacrificing of beasts upon the 25 August . . . especiallie about Lochmourie."

H

A third minute, dated "At Dingwall, 6 August 1678," relates how three generations in one family of Mackenzies—a grandfather, Hector Mackenzie of Mellan, John and Duncan his sons, and Kenneth his grandson—were summoned "for sacrificing a bull in ane heathenish manner in the iland of St Ruffus, commonly called Ellan Moury in Lochew."

Standing in silence among the graves in the dim light, with the ghostly trees all about us, and the soundless waters of the loch cutting us off from the dark hills, a mysterious aura seemed to be playing about us, and fancy filled the summer night with the lowing of an ox being led to the slaughter.

Turning to the wishing tree beside the Holy Well, we examined the coins which visitors still insert in the trunk. As we hammered in our own, we linked ourselves to the poor souls who were brought here long ago to be cured of insanity. Like St Triduana's Well at Restalrig for the curing of the blind, and St Roque's shrine at the Grange for the curing of the dreadful plague of boils, so this well on Isle Maree was credited with a magic that could cure a madness. Without either consideration or consent, the victim was bound with ropes and rowed out in a boat to the island. As he drew near he was suddenly jerked into the water of the loch, pulled in and thrown back again, a second, a third, and sometimes a fourth time, while the boat was rowed round the island. Then he was dragged ashore and compelled to drink of the waters of this well. Some rag or ribbon of the terrified patient was then tied to the tree, and an offering of money was left by his attendants.

As late as 1858 a demented young woman was brought to Isle Maree, but the cruel treatment proved

SLIOCH, LOCH MAREE

useless, and she was afterwards confined in the asylum at Inverness. In 1868, however, a furious madman was roped up and brought to the island, with two men at each end of the rope. He was dipped, and dragged as usual to the well, where he was forced to drink. Having left his offering he went home in a state of happy sanity.

It sobers the most sceptical among us to think that in the seventeenth century there were Presbyterians in Scotland who sacrificed bulls on an altar, and that less than sixty years ago lunatics were tortured by this ordeal of water at this same Isle Maree.

The well is dry now. But the tree is still laden with coins. The miracle, however, can no longer be wrought, for a shepherd from Letterewe brought a mad sheep dog to Isle Maree, half-drowned him in the loch, and then thrust him into the well. Since then the spirit of the well has departed.

But, long before the kirk had ousted the monks from Isle Maree, there lived here an aged hermit of great piety and sagacity. It was in the days when the Norsemen ruled the Western Isles and the Vikings sailed their galleys up the sea-lochs of Ross. The chief of the Vikings, Olaf, a fair-haired Prince of Norway, made his winter hermitage on one of the islands of Loch Maree. The prince fell deeply in love with a beautiful daughter of Ross, and in his dilemma sought the advice of the hermit of Isle Maree. The holy man advised him to build a tower for his bride to the west of the enclosure, where stood the monk's cell. There they were wed, and the princess stayed in the tower, while Olaf was within easy reach of his galleys in Loch Ewe. When, at last, he had to leave for a great sea-fight, there were tears on the bride's face and an ache in his own heart.

So a plan was made. When the prince returned he was to display a white flag on his galley if all was well, and a black flag if there was bad news. The princess, likewise, was to show a white or a black flag to herald her safety or distress when the Viking's galley returned.

After a long absence the Prince came back to Pool-ewe. All was well. So he stepped eagerly into his barge on Loch Maree and hoisted his snow-white flag. The Princess, during his long absence, had been tossed between despair and hope, love and jealousy. She thought that he had been untrue. With this black thought in her heart she resolved to test his love. So, when she saw the Viking's barge approaching with the white flag at the masthead, she stepped into her own little ship, hoisted the black flag, and laid herself down on a bier, all pallid as death, with a white shroud over her.

When Olaf drew near he was horrified to see his bride lying dead beneath the black flag. Leaping from the one barge to the other, he lifted the shroud, looked for a moment at the white face, drew his dirk, and plunged it into his own heart. The Princess, hearing his cry, opened her eyes, shrieked in remorse, pulled the dirk from Olaf's heart, and plunged it into her own.

The bodies of the tragic lovers were buried side by side beneath the sacred holly, and these two stones, each having a mediæval cross carved on it, mark the place of their graves to-day. All that is left of the Hermit's cell is a heap of stones, and a mound of earth close by is doubtless the site of the lover's tower. As we trace the crosses on the stones in the deepening twilight we hear that double cry of anguish out yonder on the water, and the voice of the holy man as he mutters his sacred formula, holding a crucifix before the closing eyes of the Princess.

Small wonder if the pipes were wailing as a little group of men filed slowly down to the water's edge through the gloom of the trees. For we had heard the sound of

> Old unhappy far-off things,
> And battles long ago.

As we sailed back to Talladale in the summer dark we heard another sound, like the tinkle of a smith's hammer on the anvil, and the faint sound of bellows at a forge.

" Surely some smith is working late," said some one in the boat.

" Yes—very late. For that sound is over three hundred years old ! "

May it not be that those who have the ears to hear and the spirit to understand can still catch murmurs of the old life and echoes of the daily sounds of those who lived among these mountains and along these shores ?

And the proof ?

It was in 1607 that Sir George Hay of Megginch, first Earl of Kinnoul, and the High Chancellor of Scotland, commenced iron works, or bloomeries, at Loch Maree. A *bloomery* was the first forge through which iron passed after it had been melted from the ore. It was then made into rough ingots for hammering or drawing out, and these were the *blooms*. At Letterewe, at Talladale, and at the Red Smiddy near Poolewe Sir George had his furnaces. The very name of Furnace on the shore not far from Letterewe is a lasting memorial of this ancient industry. The fuel used was wood, and all over the Highlands great forests of wood were bought

up for this purpose. Indeed, the Loch Maree furnaces
had only been going for two years when an Act of
Parliament was passed, on January 27, 1609, prohibiting
the making of iron with the natural woods of the Highlands. No wonder. For those who know tell us that
each furnace would use every year, as carbonised fuel,
the product of 120 acres of wood. In this way many
of the old Caledonian forests were cut down. These
Loch Maree works were carried on for sixty years, so
it is easy to calculate the enormous destruction of timber
in that time. As the old Act says most quaintly :
" *Forasmekle as it hes pleasit God to discover certane
vaynes of ritche mettall within this kingdome ; as alsua
certane wodis in the heylands . . . and now the estaitis
presentlie conveyned being informit that some personis . . .
wald erect yrne milnis in the same parties to the utter
waisting and consumeing of the sadis wodis . . . thairfore
the estaitis . . . ordanis . . . that nane of thame pre-
some . . . to woork and mak ony Irne with wode or
tymmer under the pane of confiscatioun of the hale yrne
that salbe maid with the said tymmer.*"

All the iron works of Loch Maree were erected by
burnsides, so the water power was probably used for
working the machinery. In the Letterfearn MS. we
read that at Letterewe " Sir George Hay kept a colony
and manufactory of Englishmen making iron and casting
great guns until the wood of it was spent and the lease
of it expired."

There must have been similar works all over the
Highlands, as those of us who have picked up relics
from the old smeltings in our wanderings know.

The industry arose during the eighteenth century.
A Liverpool company bought the woods of Glengarry
in 1730, and started iron smelting in that district. In

the same year an Irish company commenced iron smelting at Bonawe on Loch Etive. Two years later the York Buildings Company set up works at Abernethy, on Speyside. There was the Argyle Furnace Company and the Lorne Company at Inveraray. Then came Dr Roebuck, of Sheffield, William Cadell, of Cockenzie, and Samuel Garbett, of Birmingham, and established the now famous Carron Company in 1760, to be followed nineteen years later by two brothers Wilson from London, who began the Wilsontown Iron Works in Lanarkshire. In 1788 the Clyde Iron Works were started near Glasgow, and in that year there were only eight iron furnaces in Scotland.

It is a far cry from Isle Maree to the Clyde and from the charcoal burners of Ross-shire three hundred years ago to the Clydeside iron workers of to-day. But that is the meaning of the sound of the hammer on the anvil which we heard as we sailed back to Talladale from Isle Maree amid the witchery of a June night in the year of grace nineteen hundred and twenty-six.

XVII

SUDDEN SUMMER

A SUNBURST AT GAIRLOCH

I CAN always write best about heat when I am shivering with cold. For imagination is not a lying jade, as so many people seem to think. It is only that power by which man can recall, visualise, re-create, and even feel some perfectly true experience which may be long past. Do we not all enjoy reading articles about the sunshine and the flowers in dark December ? So I have always maintained that we never get the full benefit of our summer holidays until midwinter.

On these bitter days of February, when, like exiles of hope, we have all been living in Arctic conditions, it is not only good but natural to make an attempt to recapture the burning heat of the sun. A Scots summer can be bitterly disappointing, and we sometimes sigh in July for the sun. It was, therefore, in some such mood of chilled resignation that we prepared to go North last August, muttering to ourselves something about " the bitter East, the misty summer."

And then—the miracle happened !

That very morning the warm spell leaped upon us. The bell heather flamed like fire above Pitlochry. The moors of Drumouchter lay shimmering in the heat. From the heights of Drumossie we feasted our eyes on the heartsome panorama of Inverness lying in the lap

of beauty, surrounded by the fertile fields that fringe
the firth, with the massive ramparts of Wyvis beyond,
and the dim blue mountains of Ross far away. The
farther we went—by Achnasheen, Kinlochewe, Loch
Maree, and Kerrysdale—the more heat and beauty we
found, until we came to the shores of the Western sea.
It was not the least of our mercies that our windows
looked across the sea to Skye. Truly, the road that
leads north, with a slant westward to the Minch, is the
best road of all.

It was St Francis who first praised God for our
blessed brother the Sun. Here, day after day, the sun
poured down upon us a heavenly benediction of heat.
We could not escape from the fiery furnace. Sitting
on the heather, on the sands, in a boat at sea, we were
soon burned brick-red. But the very fierceness of the
sun drew forth all the most delicious scents of Nature
—a resinous whiff from the pine trees when the warm
days were windless ; the refreshing tang of bog myrtle
in the wet places of the moor ; the fragrance of honey
in the air when we plunged knee-deep through the
heather. To lie on the back and dream on such a bed
of purple was to feel the old worries slipping from the
soul. Then came summer sleep to the drone of bees.

To all this peace was added a beauty which no pen
can ever describe. The sea rippled across the golden
sands. There was a constant gluck of little waves where
the rocks cast a sheltering arm round the bay. The
shallows were iridescent with every shade of amber,
amethyst, and green. The majestic Ross-shire hills—
Boshven and Alligan—looked ethereal and unreal in the
heat haze, and the long elusive line of Skye lay like a
cloud on the rim of the horizon. And when the burning
day was done the sun went down behind the little moors

of Strath, not with the flaming glories which so often
make the Western sky tragic after a day of storm, but
with a holy quietness that filled the heart like an evening
benediction. Then the blue-dusk sky, with a star or
two, and the cool oblivion of sleep.

When the days became insufferably warm we crawled
along to the sands. The glistering beaches, someone has
called them. Here was sea-water that was cool enough
to be refreshing, yet warm enough to give pleasure.
Down in the holy hollow of the *Leabaidh*—that green
bed in the dunes where for generations the good folks
of Gairloch sat at the white tables and remembered
Christ—not a breath of wind tempered the heat. But
beyond the dunes lie the sands, and where the golden
circle ends the rocks make a paradise for those who swim.

Who can describe this most blessed of all summer
delights ? Standing erect in the blazing sun, arms
raised for the adventurous plunge, a rush of liquid
music in the ears as the green depths are explored, and
sheer buoyancy brings us up to the sunlight again.

> Cold throbs of life, light as the bubbles surging
>   From the swift encircling hand ;
> On throat and hair the quivering ice-stars breaking
>   Like foam of silver wine ;
> Waves of exulting thought in sense awaking
>   Glamour of youth divine.
>
> Welcome the breathless marge ! the sunlight burning
>   From new caressing skies !
> A luxury of rest in warmth returning,
>   Laughter for clearer eyes.
>
>   G. WINTHROP YOUNG.

Surrounded by youth and its care-free laughter in
this place of mermaid pleasures, it was easy to recapture

the heart of a boy, and to forget that there was any such thing as care in all the happy world.

One day I sat high up amid the waste of bogs and moors that lie above North Erradale. Here the silence of death seemed to reign. From this point the view is wide and wonderful. The mountains of Torridon rise to the south, the great hunch of Liagach, and the mighty tops of Ben Eighe. I could see the loom of the Applecross hills above the long flat line of moors that run out to Red Point. Rona, Raasay, and Northern Skye floated in the misty silence. The heat was too great to make it possible to see the Outer Isles. One boat lay becalmed on the shining sea. Longay, like a bottle-nosed whale, rose from the water in the near distance. There was no sign of life, no sound, only an occasional whisper of mysterious airs about the ears. All nature seemed to have swooned, and the silence rang across the moors like a little bell of God to recall a wanderer to a sense of eternal things. Then a solitary whaup cried eerily, as if seeking its lost mate. Far away in a croft at Erradale a cock crowed. The whole landscape seemed to cry out of the dead old days when this world of bogs and mountains was one vast forest, with a race of Celtic heroes fighting blood feuds among the trees, and living on the bare bones of existence. At any moment ghosts of the past might peer at you from behind the hummocks and lichen-covered boulders. That very bunch of red-pine roots at my feet, which has been gathered from the peat haggs, is part of the primeval forest through which the wild boars routed after their food. Here is the blessing of the separate. For, as the old blind gangrel said to me long ago :

" You can never win close to things till you climb

high, all your lone, where there is nobody else to break the thrum."

It was a long, hot descent to the shore at Carn Dearg, in the blazing sun. But a plunge into the cool green sea, the pine roots burning brightly on the hot rocks, and there was peace and plenty by the edge of the whispering tide.

Even on the water it was hard to find coolness. For the glassy sea threw back the heat as from the surface of a burnished mirror. The old boat chug-chugged its way across the mouth of the Kerry river, past the bay of Shieldaig, between the isle of Horrisdale and the tiny land-locked village of Badachro, and right out to the tilted rocks of Opinan. We found a delicious well on the shore, with an old causeway leading to it, and here the blue reek was soon rising into the still air.

There is a flat rock that shelves into the deep water near Shieldaig Bay. It is called the *Leac-nan-saighead*, or the Slab of the Arrow. And this is the tale you will hear at the *ceilidh*.

As far back as 1480 a commission of fire and sword was granted by the king to Hector Roy Mackenzie to exterminate the Gairloch Macleods. Be very sure the Macleods bitterly resented being expelled from Gairloch, for they never were a small-souled clan. So they sat for a time in the hall at Dunvegan brooding revenge. It was then that Fair-haired Sarah, an old Skye *cailleach* with the sight, urged them on to go back and gain their own again on the shores of Ross. Up they sprang and crowded into the black birlinn. It was the dusk of day when they sailed into Gairloch, and night when they landed on little Fraoch Eilean. There they hid themselves till morning.

But Donald and Ian Odhar, the famous Macrae

archers, had spied on their coming. So they stole round the shores in the deep of night to *Leac-nan-saighead*. The flat Slab of the Arrow overlooks Fraoch Eilean. Standing on the step of this rock, yet concealed from any one watching from the island, the Macrae archers began to shoot at dawn. Some of the Macleods were killed before they found out the spot from which the deadly arrows came. Then their comrades began to return the fire. But their arrows were only splintered on the *Leac-nan-saighead*. At last one of the Macleods, in exasperation, climbed the mast of the birlinn, to get a better view of the enemy. Ian Odhar saw him, fitted an arrow to his string, and nailed the Macleod to the mast.

"You have sent a pin through his broth!" said Donald Odhar.

So the slaughter went on until only two Macleods escaped in the birlinn. For the rest, trenches were dug on the island, and to-day you can see the green howes.

Sad tales, with blood in every one of them.

Now, alas, the sun has gone. The weather is broken. The clouds are down on Skye. There is a tang of autumn in the air. A robin is singing his plaintive song in the woods at Flowerdale—that song which always means good-bye to summer. The night closes in with a steady downpour of rain, and the wind moans eerily about the chimneys on the Hill of Treasure. But we have had our sunburst, and are content to rest our souls in memory.

XVIII

GLEN TORRIDON

AND THE ROAD TO DIABAIG

It is useless to ask what is the finest glen in Scotland. Glens are like people. Each has its own character, its own scenery, its own beauty, and its own history.

So with Glen Torridon. No other glen could be mistaken for it. But it is something of an adventure to describe a region whose very road lies along the oldest floor in the world. Wild, desolate, remote—it is all that, this unpeopled glen where an occasional rickle of stones cries out of a race that is now no more. When you have used up all the adjectives, there is something more about Torridon—an indescribable something which grips you with a sense of the unutterable.

The glen, moreover, has a lonely outgait to the Western sea. At first sight Loch Torridon seems to be nothing but a land-locked lake, with the blue line of the Skye hills above its rather low shores. But when you look down from the hills above Alligan and Diabaig, Torridon is a mountain-encircled arm of the sea, eleven miles long from the little Ploc at its head to Rhu na Fearn at its mouth, with three distinct reaches—the Upper Loch, Loch Shieldaig, and Loch Torridon proper —slanting northwards to the Minch.

The bounds of Torridon can be described in one

LIATHACH FROM GLEN TORRIDON

bald paragraph. The loch is exactly the same length as the glen, which is dominated by two great mountains —Ben Eighe and Liagach. If you have travelled from Achnasheen down Glen Dochartie, you will find the road to Torridon striking off to the left just beyond Kinlochewe, and all the way to the sea it never rises above 400 feet. About four miles along this desolate road lies lovely Loch Clair on the south side, and you get a glimpse of Coulin Lodge among the trees, with Scuir Dubh and the mountains of Coulin forest behind. These are the bounds of Glen Torridon.

But who can describe this silent glen, which is one of the oldest ante-chambers of the world! Travelling on this roadway, you are passing over one of the first foundations of the earth. For these great mountains of Torridon sandstone rise directly from a primeval bed of gneiss.

Not many weeks ago, when passing through Torridon, I tried to explain to a Highlander the age of his own glen, for his oft-repeated questions demanded an answer :

" How did the like o' that big rock get there ? "

" How were the like o' these cliffs made ? "

" If the ice made these scratches, why are there no frosts and ice the like o' that now ? "

So I pointed to Liagach. For I know no mountain in Scotland which gives us a more instant sense of the age of the earth. It stands on the oldest rock in the world. It rises steeply from the roadway. Its walls represent unimaginable ages of creation. Yet, from its roots in the primeval gneiss, up these terrific sandstone terraces to the very top of its white quartzite cap, the eye can take in at a glance the whole three thousand feet of ageless masonry.

Liagach rising sheer
  From river-bed up to the sky,
Grey courses of masonry tier on tier,
  And pinnacles splintered on high.

Splintered, contorted, and riven,
  As though, from the topmost crown
Some giant plougher his share had driven
  In a hundred furrows sheer down.

                              PRINCIPAL SHAIRP.

The sandstone cliffs tell us of God's first great seas,
and of the æons of time which must have elapsed ere
these grim precipices were slowly deposited, grain by
grain, and shelf by shelf. How often, after that, must
the earth have been rocked to its primal founds, with
mighty upheavals that cracked and twisted and crumpled
the strata, sending tremendous overthrusts of one rocky
world on to the top of another ! Then came the age of
ice, when this unpeopled land was slowly ground down,
and carved out into glens and corries. The waters of
the melted ice gradually receded, and now these smooth
and deeply scratched surfaces remain to this day on the
level places of Maree and Torridon. Truly, Liagach
must have taken an eternity to build. And yet that was
only a little bit of time !

Take your stand on any viewpoint of these hills, and
if the visibility is good, your eye, ranging over Ross and
Sutherland, will pick up a great many mountains of
similar form which pierce the sky like pyramids—Quinag,
Canisp, Suilven, Cul Mhor, the Coygach hills, the
Teallach mountains in the Dundonnell forest, Slioch,
Ben Eighe, Liagach—all children of the same primeval
family, standing like silent sentinels of time which have
withstood the desolations of incalculable ages.

And what colour the Almighty Artist has lavished on these ancient hills !

The blues and greys of the original gneiss, the warm hues of the sandstone terraces, the gleam of the white quartzite caps. I have seen them steeped in the light of the setting sun, the lower rocks all blue with shadows in the mystic twilight of the glen, the red cliffs glowing in the level rays, and the cones of snow lifting their heads majestically to catch the last beams of the dying day.

> Benyea, magnificent alp,
> Blanched bare and bald and white,
> His forehead like old sea eagle's scalp,
> Seen athwart the sunset light !

To view these Torridon mountains in the silence of a summer night—from a boat on Loch Maree, from the Bridge of Grudie, from the shores of Loch Clair, or from some point in Glen Torridon itself—is to be overawed with a sense of the wonder of the world and the age of the earth. For these are the

> Regions consecrate to oldest time.

On the south side of Glen Torridon lies the Corrie of a Hundred Hills. It is so-called because of a vast number of rounded, heather- and grass-covered hillocks which lie there. These little moraine dumps, which geologists call *roches moutonnées*, or rocky sheepbacks, are also a legacy from the melted ice of the glaciers.

Very often in a glen, or on the level floor of a Highland valley, you will see these rounded mounds standing there, bare and green, or covered with trees. The Celts call them Shians, or Fairy Knolls. If the wee folks still hold their revels in the remote places of the north, calling strangely from below and making compelling music

I

which no mortal can with safety listen to, then the Corrie of a Hundred Hills must be a weird place for wandering, either in a summer gloaming or in the mirk of a winter forenight.

Come to Torridon any way you please, you will come to the end of a lonesome world. There is here no through-going road. A motorist cannot take Torridon in the passing. It is a bit of unspoiled mountain solitude. The road ends at the gates of Torridon House. At the very head of the loch there is a fine example of a *cairidh*, set across the tidal way from shore to shore. Here, when the tide recedes, the fish are imprisoned. Between the village and the lodge gate a slab of stone stands by the roadside to keep green the memory of a beloved laird. The inscription is as follows :

" This stone was erected in 1912 by Ann, widow of Duncan Darroch, of Gourock and Torridon, in memory of the devotion and affection shown by one hundred men on the estate of Torridon, who, at their own request, carried his body from the house here on its way to interment in the family burial place at Gourock."

Would that every proprietor in the Highlands to-day knew his people and was loved by them like that !

> See that thou kindly use them, O man !
>   To whom God giveth
> Stewardship over them in thy short span,
>   Not for thy pleasure !
> Woe be to them who choose for a clan
>   Four-footed people !
>   ALEX. NICOLSON.

By the goodwill of all concerned, the old right-of-way has just been restored from the lodge gate along the shore to the isolated village of Alligan. How much this means to the dwellers in Upper and Lower Alligan will be well understood when I describe the alternative road which leads over the hills for seven miles to Diabaig.

It is one of the wildest and most soul-satisfying hill roads I know, rising and falling about 1000 feet in a few miles, with some sensational gradients, a bad surface, hairpin bends to suit the taste of a trick rider, no passing places to speak of, and a hill as bad at the end as at the beginning. The road to Diabaig is a hill walker's ideal track. But it was my good fortune to drive over it in a little four-seater, with a lady at the wheel whose nerve is just as fine as her driving ability.

Near the top of the worst hill I was quite prepared to jump. Coming down this same hill on the return journey you have a clear view of the sea, 800 feet below, as if the bottom of the road, but, mercifully, there is a hairpin bend just there, so you go round and not over. On the top level, where the road runs through the wild Bealach na Gaoithe, or the Windy Gowl, there are wonderful views from the shore of a little hill loch. Then the road once more takes a nasty dive for half a mile down a stony surface, with a bankless drop of several hundred feet to a solitary sheet of fresh water—Loch Diabaig Airde. A mile or so of easy going along the shores of this loch and we once more topped the rise which is above Loch Diabaig itself, where there is another truly testing hill down to the village on the seashore.

The return journey—always a thought—was just as exhilarating. But to those who would drive to Diabaig let me say three things—pray that your flight be not in bad weather, else the road will be like the bed of a stream; that you have not to turn back, because you cannot; and that you meet no other car either on the

breast or the back of the bad hills, for then, like the two
goats on the plank bridge, you must either go back or
go over.

We stopped at a turning-place above Diabaig, and
lit a fire for lunch. A stalker who had heard of our
coming walked for an hour before he found us there.
Here time and distance are as nothing. There on the
heather, by the remains of the fire, we held one of the
finest of *ceilidhs*.

There are days which are so heavenly that to win
their glories all risks are justifiable. The whole world
of Torridon lay about us—the great solitudes of Ben
Alligan ; the summer sea flashing in the sun right over
to the shores of Rona, Raasay, and Skye ; the Applecross mountains across the loch ; Shieldaig tucked away
on its own loch, where the road goes up the glen and
over the hills to Kishorn ; Loch Damph worming its
way into the forest. The peace of the day fell on us
like a benediction as we feasted our eyes on the far
horizons, recognising the bens and glens and islands as
only those can who have loved them for a lifetime. We
heard some old-time tales of the passes through these
hills, and of the dool of those who long ago had fought
their battles there. But memory only recalls the peace,
the beauty, and the happiness of that day

—the mountain Sabbath that ever more
a sanctuary here doth keep.

XIX

THE OLD ROAD TO THE TIGH DIGE

OR THE ART OF WALKING SLOW

THIRTY-FIVE miles in one day is certainly good walking, and the first time I tramped this Kerrysdale road we kept up a speed of four miles an hour. But we were young then, and there were one or two things we did not know. One of them was, that slow-going is not always unheroic.

In this age of hurry, when most of us spend our time rushing about the world from one place to another, and an absent-minded pedestrian is not safe on a high road, we are beginning to realise that there is a great deal more than luck in leisure. That is why the old by-paths in the country are coming back to their own, where the contemplative man can walk in peace, and the poor soul who has been run off his feet in a city can look, and loiter, and listen to his heart's content.

You strike the old road as you cross the hills from Loch Maree to Gairloch. It begins at the Red Stable, on the shores of little Loch Bad na Scalaig, and wanders for miles among the moors, until it drops down opposite the old Tigh Dige at Flowerdale.

A derelict woodman's shack stands near the point where the track leaves the Kerrysdale road. A forsaken dwelling always fires the imagination. As we pass in at the open door one or two sheep scamper out and rush

along the tiny veranda. When all the woods were
waving in the wind up here this must have been a fine
forester's shanty. But now! The great double stove
in the main apartment is a rusted ruin : the paper is
hanging from the walls ; a bunch of holly all withered
and dry hangs from the roof, a pathetic relic of the last
Christmas carousal. The whole place smells of decay.
So we pass out and look round rather sadly on that
which is now a common sight in the Highlands—a
whole hill-side cleared of timber, with no sign of new
woods taking the place of the old.

The road, which is covered in places with fine old
turf, has been well built, as the ancient stone foundations
at the corners show. The blessedness of an old road is,
that it always leads you into a sanctuary of solitude.
Up here there are no sounds but the sough of wandering
winds, the whisper of little streams, and the drone of
an industrious bee as it flits from one heather tuft to
another. Gorgeous dragon-flies dart across the path ;
butterflies flutter above the heather ; great purple-
headed beetles rush about among the grasses on nimble
legs ; little stick insects alight on the rocks, like tiny
bits of bark, and rest themselves with that perfect
mimicry for which Mother Nature is proverbial ; a big
grasshopper with green armoured thorax, goggle eyes,
and a most comical mouth, suns itself on a stone, its
mighty legs cocked up like the cantilevers of a bridge.
You have only to sit down by the old road, and look
largely at Nature with your own eyes, or with a minuter
vision through a pocket microscope, to see all that and
a great deal more.

Then the track descends through a narrow little
gorge, with a tiny stream flowing by the side of the
green road, which is made beautiful here by a few

birch trees. The music of that running water would soothe the soul of the most anxious. To wander thus in such a world, alert yet unhasting, is the only way to win the blessing of the loiterer. The far-off hoot of a motor reminds me of the words of one who himself has been an exquisite exponent of the refinements of loitering :

> Of speed, the savour and the sting,
>   None but the weak deride :
> But, ah, the joy of lingering
>   About the countryside !
> The swiftest wheel, the conquering run,
>   We count no privilege
> Beside acquiring, in the sun,
>   The secret of the hedge.

E. V. Lucas.

There speaks the wise wanderer who does not despise speed when it is necessary, but who knows also the true value of leisure. A rhapsody of sauntering, a gloria of ease ; the delicate and gentle art of never getting there—these are some of the word poems of this most refined of loiterers who has given a whole generation the benefit of what his own quiet eyes have seen.

The pathway now opens out along the mountain side, with wide views across Shieldaig forest, and one heartsome glimpse of the blue sea. At this point the road runs over a bit of flat glacier-worn rock. Another little shelving rock rises from the side of the path, with a heather bank above. Here is the obvious place for the midday meal. A fire is soon blazing against the upright rock. The reek rises against the grey bluff, and so disperses itself as to be invisible to the eye of a watcher. It is sheer luxury to lie in the heat, and do nothing but look and listen. What first-hand pleasures are here ! The generous sunshine, the wide views of moors and mountains, midday peace, the husheen of invisible waters, two tramps who know what not to say, a simple meal, and a whiff of fragrant coffee. Add to this natural pleasure-house of God, the purple heather all honey-scented, the russet hues of birch and bracken, the dull gold of fading mosses, and the glory is manifold.

After this the road swings round a corner and descends into a green hollow, where great trees stand on the old turf meadows. Nestling among the trees is a clachan of thatched houses, with one white-washed cottage. One of the trees by the roadside is a very old larch, with mighty arms that reach out and upwards, as is the habit of ancient larches. Looking at this majestic tree, one naturally thinks of the huge larches at Meggernie Castle, Monzie Castle, and Dunkeld House, for these were among the first larches to be planted in this country.

Sitting in this green glade, under the immemorial trees, a man of vision might dream through the livelong day, calling to mind tales of old-time travellers, or cavalcades of Highland retainers following the laird and his lady on their fine little garrons, with little children strapped into creels, as they all make their way down to the old Tigh Dige, which was the chief's dwelling-place.

To hurry here would be sacrilege. To leave the glade and climb the next stage of the journey, past a little forest of pines and birches, takes but a few minutes. But a great beech tree at the top of the rise offers another delightful temptation, for there are good temptations as well as bad in this alluring world. And the heat is an immediate excuse. What welcome shade these mighty beech branches afford ! The wind sends a refreshing swish through the myriad leaves, and, as we listen, a phrase of Robert Louis Stevenson lingers in the memory :

Green days in forests.

No matter how heavy the bundle on your back may be, or how sweltering the heat, cool pleasures will blow through you here.

And the history of the road keeps marching on before your eyes. Wild Macleods and wild Mackenzies, hurrying to the foray, and waging their little wars, between the sea and the hills. Generations of ghostly men and little children. Raiders from the isles or the hostile shires, stealing silently down the old road, when the moon has dipped behind Boshven, and there is a stillness like death in the glen. But, when they hurry up the road again, driving cattle before them, and carrying their wounded, there is red ruin in the clachan and the sound of keening, where the scattered homesteads stand smoking in the morning sun.

But it is time to go again. So we descend reluctantly into the more civilised region of Flowerdale—a beautiful place with an unpardonable English name. Here are plantations and pine trees, a river, and a glimpse of the chimneys of the Tigh Dige smoking among the trees. On the way down you pass a ruined cottage on the farther side of the glen. Four grey walls and two gaping gables stand on the braeface, with the woods and rocks of Sithean Mhor and Groban making a splendid background. It is the picture of what has been and what will never be again in these remote Highlands—a heartbreaking coronach in stone.

Then the woodman's yards, and evidence of those new Highland clearances which began with the Great

War. Across the stream is the ancient Island of Justice, now a green mound, close by the place on which stood the original Tigh Dige, or stank house, of the Mackenzies. And here at last is what was once the Old Inn, by the side of the bridge where the river falls into the sea. With the yellow wrack the old road comes to an end. But just round the corner, when you top the rise of the new road which leads to the north, the green hollow of Leabaidh na Ba Baine, or Bed of the White Cow, lies at your feet. When you lift your eyes from that hallowed spot you will catch a glimpse of the Hebrid Isles lying like a cloud on the rim of the shining sea.

XX

PREACHING CAVES

BY THE WESTERN SEA

IT is many years since I first stood in the oldest preaching cave in Scotland and took a drawing of the little crosses which are carved on its rocky wall. After a good trudge from Whithorn, I found the cave of St Ninian beneath a samphire-covered cliff on the shores of Luce Bay, not far from Glasserton and Monreith. As Ninian came to this district some time in the fourth century, tradition, if not authentic history, has associated his name with the cave for over fifteen hundred years. That is enough to make any man of imagination thrill with holy thoughts as he stands alone in this remote spot and fingers the little crosses.

When Dean Stanley was preparing his lectures on the history of the Church of Scotland, he stayed at Monreith, and visited this Hermit's Haunt in 1871. On that occasion an incised cross was found on the west side of the entrance. Within the next few years other crosses were found, and after several feet of rubbish had been cleared away a stone pavement was revealed. On one of the paving stones a rudely-cut inscription was discovered, of which this fragment was clearly made out : SANCT NI . . . P.

Since fingering these crosses in St Ninian's cave I have travelled many roads and visited many crosses and caves, from grey Galloway to the far Orkneys, and yet, when standing in any primitive place of preaching, my thoughts always fly back to this Hermit's Haunt on the Bay of Luce.

Not many years after that I came upon another preaching cave farther north, by the shores of green Argyll. This time I knew and talked with the lay preacher who had transformed his cave into a rude chapel—John Campbell of Ledaig, the Bard of Benderloch. But, alas, none will ever enter this preaching cave again, for, when the railway was pushed beyond Loch Etive, the cave was altogether destroyed.

Beneath the huge rock nestled the thatched cottage of John Campbell. Nature and the soft climate of Argyll have greatly favoured this little bit of legendary land, and his garden was prodigal with fruits and flowers—mimulus, pansies, rosemary, sweet william, convolvulus, and heaps of roses grew side by side. Through his beloved flowers came the Bard to offer welcome. He was a man of medium height, well up in years, with keenly-cut Celtic features, and a mild, beautiful eye. It was a pleasant thing to listen to the lilt of the soft voice, but pleasanter still to think of the man who lived and wrote and preached for forty years in this far-away retreat.

Crossing the road we entered another garden which had been made by his own hand, on the top of a large rocky platform. At the foot of this bluff the sea was breaking. Wending our way through the flowers, we followed him down some steps in the very centre of the garden to a low-placed door. Passing through the door, we found ourselves in a large rock-hewn cave. A small window faced the sea, and gave glorious views of Mull. At one end there was a rudely-built fireplace, with a shelf or two of books, and at the other end stood a table made from an oak tree under which Robert Bruce is said to have rested after the Battle of Bannockburn. All round the walls were wooden benches sufficient to accommodate fifty people. The floor of the cave was laid with planks of wood.

This cave was the poet's chapel. Here he preached the Word for the best part of a lifetime, and taught the younger people of the district knowledge of the great things of life. Often as the little company sat to hear or stood to sing, the breakers would pound against the rocks and drench the window with spray. Here came not only the neighbours in winter-time to worship, but here also came many great folks in summer to visit the Bard, as a glance at his visitors' book revealed. John Stuart Blackie was a frequent friend. For John Campbell himself wrote much poetry, both in Gaelic and in English. He lived all his life at Dunvalanree, where Ossian held his Feast of Shells, in music-haunted Selma, by the shores of the sounding sea.

But these things all belong to the past. The Bard is long since dead. The rock on the shore, the garden, and the cave itself have all been blasted away. But the memory of it remains, like a whiff of rosemary, fragrant and haunting.

From the time of St Ninian down to times which are within the memory of one or two who are still living, Scots folk have had to worship God in some strange places. But, the more they were opposed, the more determined were they to seek out some natural sanctuary. The most Mosaic place of worship known to me was not a cave, but the Floating Kirk of Loch Sunart—that long arm of the sea which separates Ardnamurchan from the storied land of Morven.

In 1843, when the people of Sunart could obtain no site from the proprietor for a place of worship, they conceived the novel idea of having a floating tabernacle which could be anchored out in the loch, where no landlord could prohibit. At a cost of £2000 a huge iron hulk was built on the Clyde and fitted out with a pulpit, benches, and a small vestry. The ship had comfortable sitting accommodation for 750 people. This extraordinary kind of Noah's Ark was towed all the way from the Clyde, round the Mull of Kintyre, and up the stormy west coast to Loch Sunart, by one or two tug-boats. Sometimes the floating kirk was crowded. At all times the attendance was registered by a scale of feet marked on the stern of the boat, so that a very little arithmetic was needed to determine whether there were four, five, or seven hundred people at worship on a Sunday. Occasionally, when a storm sprang up during a service, both preachers and listeners were greatly moved.

There never was a ship constructed on the Clyde so like the Ark as the Floating Kirk of Loch Sunart, with its bluff barge-like foundation, its whole deck space filled with a square house, having sloping roof, windows fore and aft, and in both port and starboard sides.

There still exists a picture of its arrival in the loch, with the setting sun behind the tug-boat towing the Ark of the Covenant, while two black-coated men stand on the shore and marvel at the curious spectacle. Here was the same spirit that made men gather in caves and dens of the earth to worship God when no stately temple was available.

Recently I came on two other primitive temples on the shores of Wester Ross.

The first is near the township of Sand of Udrigil,

on the beautiful bay of Gruinard. You take the road from Poolewe past Aultbea, and cross the moors by Laid. The views across Gruinard on a fine summer day are nothing short of celestial. Just before dropping down to the shores of Gruinard you pass on the left the ruined Chapel of Sand of Udrigil, an ancient holy place standing in a crowded graveyard, and then a little way along the road you come to a well-marked path, all grass-grown now, but once a causeway leading to the shore.

Follow this old road and it will lead you down some rough stone-built steps to a shingle beach, where the great waves break, sucking the pebbles down with a rattle as each roller recedes. Weird stacks of rock stand out of the water like rugged sentinels. Here you will find a large cave which has been hollowed out by the restless waves in a crack of the sandstone cliff. A little wall is built in front of it, but the entrance is quite open now, although it was once fitted with a doorway which had a lock and key.

Long ago this cave was used by the worshippers of the Free Church. It is large and roomy, receding far into the cliff, but the inner part is low and difficult of access. What a romantic spot for worship, with the sea breaking upon the pebbly beach in sunshine or storm! Many a time the preacher must have had to raise his voice to overcome the sound of the pounding seas.

Alongside of this preaching cave you will find a smaller one. Here, for a long time, an old woman lived with a girl for her companion. Her fire was on the left by the entrance, the bed was on the right, and the front was built up with stones and turf. The only literature which the old woman possessed was a Gaelic Bible.

But the most complete specimen of a preaching cave known to me is far up the west side of Loch Ewe. The road from Poolewe wanders for eight miles northwards along the shore. Here is an absolutely unspoiled bit of crofting country, and the very names of the townships through which you pass have a sough of those Norse and Celtic races which mingled their blood here in far-off times. Boor, Naust, Inverasdale, Smo, Mellan Gauna, Cove—all well-kept, bien-looking crofts, with good houses, and here and there a bunch of Highland shelties on the heather. The road is narrow, and there are six or eight gates to open and shut between Poolewe and Cove. But to me that only adds merit to this road, for here you are perfectly safe from the racing motorist or the eyeless tripper who speeds from hotel to hotel in search of food.

At Smo there is a beautiful bay with a sweep of yellow sand. About a mile farther on you come to another bay called Camus allt Eoin Thomais. Beyond this lies the township of Cove, which is a scatter of cosy crofts behind a bluff headland called Sron-nan-oban, or the Nose of the Little Bay.

Cross the hayfield between the road and the sea, follow the path through a flowery meadow till you come to some steep natural stone steps, and you will find yourself on a shore of shingle and rugged rocks. Turn to the left, and the dark opening in the rocks, screened by greenery and ferns, is the entrance to the cave.

It is a wide, roomy, high-roofed cave, and you descend into it by one or two stone steps. But the unique feature of this cave is, that a wooden pulpit still stands on the north side, faced by a row of rough wooden benches, with bookboards attached. There

BEINN EIGHE FROM LOCH COULIN

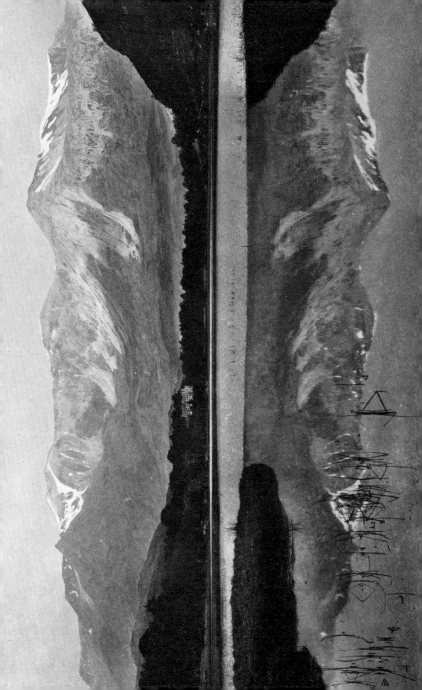

must have been more seats at one time, and I am told there was a wooden floor. The entrance is roughly built up with stones in the usual way, and little festoons of ferns hang from the roof.

What a picture the imagination paints as you stand and look round ! You see the preacher in the pulpit, and the people on the benches, within this strange rock temple not made with hands. You hear the wail of the Gaelic psalms, the lilted line, and the chorus of men's and women's voices singing in solemn unison. Outside, the waves are breaking with a holy husheen on the sun-lit shores, and the far view of the blue mountains makes a finer parable of heaven than any words of a preacher ever can. How long the pulpit and the benches have stood there, or when the last sermon was preached in this hallowed spot, I cannot say. But in the silence of this cave there is still a sound of Gaelic singing to those who have an ear which leans fondly to the drones of time.

But I have memories of more than that at Cove on the shores of Ewe.

I can still see the spotless interior of the cottage where the kettle was boiled ; the pure white walls and rafters ; the snowy fireplace where the peats were blazing ; and the kettle hung on the sworlie. I can see also the unrivalled range of hills in Ross and Suther-land—that unbroken panorama of peaks, dim and elusive, from the point of Stoer and Suilven to the giants of Torridon—Eighe, Liagach, and Alligan. I can see the bright green machair lands of Ewe, the yellow sands and the sparkling seas at my feet, as I stand on the height of Sron-nan-oban and watch the waves grum-bling below me on the black rocks, or surging through the natural archway of a great stack. I can see the old

K

derelict house on the roadside with its curious crow-stepped gable, abandoned as if some sudden plague had stricken the tenants. The quaint wooden canopy over the fire ; the swee still in its place ; dishes left on the dresser ; a table, a stool, and a settle overturned ; the wooden shot-bolt in the door ; the straw-strewn floors ; and the very picture-cords hanging from the walls !

It was our last day in Ross. But, amid all the sun-shine and beauty, the laughter and pleasant company, I could hear the end of an old song, and the last long drawn-out notes of a pibroch. A sea wind blew about us as we turned to look back, and the very breeze seemed to be laden with lost notes :

> O wind, O mighty, melancholy wind,
>   Blow through me, blow !
> Thou blowest forgotten things into my mind,
>   From long ago.

> TODS HUNTER.

XXI

THE FINDING OF RED RIVER

AN ADVENTURE IN FRIENDSHIP

I LOST him on a lochside years ago, somewhere in the region of Tummel and Rannoch. He was an orra man *de luxe*, the complete ghillie, an all-round sportsman, with a few other talents that need not be mentioned. We took to each other at the first glance, before we were prejudiced by names or any such trivial personalities. Indeed, if there were no social ranks in this conventional world, but only human affinities, some of us would be oxtering queer characters.

His real name was Willie. But we called him Red River, because he had spent some years on a ranch in the Red River Settlements. His stories of Red Indians would make a boy's hair stand on end. He had also been in the Army, in the Navy, in the American Rockies, and on the veldt in South Africa. I find in an old notebook something about taking a deer noiselessly with a hook and a bunch of corn. But the details of this extraordinary proceeding would not be profitable either to the public or to the proprietor of a deer forest. The note, however, was evidently written after my first meeting with Red River, although it is not always safe, even for a Scot, to draw an inference.

After my departure on that occasion my host asked Red River what he thought I was. He made a guess at several brilliant occupations, but in every case was wide of the mark. When at last the real truth was told him, his conscience smote him painfully as he ran over some of our private conversations ; but, regaining himself, he said with a reckless twinkle in his eye :

"Well, it disna matter ; he was a cheerie devil, anyway ! "

From that day to this I have loved Red River, and have looked for him up and down Scotland. But he was too independent a gangrel to stay long in any one spot of earth. So, at last, I had to write him down on the tablet of my memory as—" Gone—leaving no address."

Last summer I was wandering all alone on a Ross-shire road which skirts the shore and has a fine view of Skye. Between the road and the sea a little wooden shack stands on the turf. Many a time I looked in at the window, and the oftener I looked the more I was interested. It was so small, so tidy, and so evidently occupied by a man who had a place for everything, but who lived the frugal life of a solitary. On this particular day I met a young collie that I did not know, and was bending over the dog in a long conversation. A shadow fell on the road, and when I looked up I saw that an elderly man had come out of the shack. He stood there staring at me with a most beatific smile on his face.

"Do you no' mind of me, sir ? "

"Red River !   Red River ! " I cried.

Men certainly were not given faces for nothing.

"I knew you were here, sir.   For I heard the pipes. But have you brought yon wee catapult ? "

I answered Red River with one eye, pulled something out of my doublet, and in a moment we were

A BLACK HOUSE

inside the shack like brother conspirators. Then the *ceilidh* began, and it was as if the years between Rannoch and Ross had never been.

He had come back, like many another Highlander, after a lifetime's wanderings, to end his days on the old family croft. He built this shack on the shore, and so kept his independence ; but he was also within cry of the old roof-tree where his mother had taught him to toddle ; so he was at home. There are Celts, like himself, who have wandered to the ends of the earth. Some of them come back again, and some never return. But not one of them can think of the old home without a yearning to be there. So, with an old boat, Red River pursues his ancient trade of fisherman in the waters where he first caught flukies with a rusty hook and a home-made line. He had broken his arm some weeks previous to this, but he is a clean healer, and it did not seem to incommode him unless when he was heaving the anchor. He bathes in the sea all through the summer and winter. When the shores are gripped with frost, the crofters, who are not lovers of cold water, say to each other :

" Look you—Willie must be wanting to die."

But Red River has no thought of dying. He is full of the joy of living. He has only learned the secrets of good health—fresh air, plenty of exercise, cold water, and frugal feeding. So, to-day, he is a whippy old man, with apple cheeks and a clear eye. But, after all his wanderings, he has come home.

What stories must be told in that little shack by the sea on the dark winter nights when the tiny bench by the fire is crowded, and the place is full of tobacco reek, and the tale goes round, and another peat is thrown on the fire ! Old escapades when they were all boys in the little school along the lochside. Great stories of the fishing at sea, of deer on the hill, of the long desolate moorlands to the north where the black bothies are still so hard to find, and of dark nights spent silently at the river mouth over yonder, where only yesterday I saw a silver salmon splashing in the sun.

But the story I like best is his tale of the Red Indian horse thief.

Sixteen horses were missing from the ranch. Red River and two other cowboys were sent to track the thief and round up the horses. Each took a different route over the hills, with one day's rations. They were away for three days without getting on the track of the thief. At last Red River reined in his horse on a rocky summit and scanned the lower ground. He noticed a white spot a good way off. Just then two bullets whizzed past his ear. Raising his rifle he fired at the white spot, but it moved off. Then he fired at a dark spot alongside. There was no reply after that. So he rode down and found the sixteen horses hidden behind some rocks. The dark spot was the wounded Indian, who lay scowling at him, while his white horse grazed peacefully by his side. Red River attended to the wounded man, rounded up the horses, and took the long trail home. The other two cowboys found the Indian later on, and robbed him of three hundred dollars. When they reached the ranch they waved the money in Red River's face with a laugh. He felt a bit sore, but bided his time.

Very soon after that they were sent out to find eleven horses that had been stolen. But, before leaving the ranch, Red River dealt with the two cowboys separately. Covering each in turn with his revolver, he gabbled Gaelic curses over them and made each hand him fifty dollars. So he got his own back, and on this second trek there was no plunder.

One day I trysted Red River to go afishing with us. His way with fish was wonderful, and he knew every bank in the loch. After pulling fish into the old boat almost to weariness, we began to talk of the birds. It was a perfectly calm afternoon. One bird was sailing on the water a considerable way off.

" Could you hit that one, sir ? "

It was a long shot, and I pulled out the catapult with fear and trembling, lest I should fail before the old man. But in all cases of high emergency the only thing to do is to appear utterly indifferent. So I selected my best stone, raised the sling, did not hang on the aim, and let fly. We all heard the thud of the stone against the bird. Red River was wild with excitement, but no one got a greater surprise than myself. I had the sense, however, not to try again, and put away the deadly weapon with supreme indifference.

When we got to the shore, his nephew was waiting to help us with the fish. Red River poured out a perfect epic on the catapult, and ended his fiery description with this generous hyperbole :

" Yes, and he never misses. He never misses ! "

Having won this utterly false reputation, I slunk home with the fish, a very humble man.

O Red River ! I am far from the shack on the shores of Ross. But you are like many another wayfaring man whom I have met on that road which none can ever err in loving. You have heard the call that many an exiled heart is hearing to-night, in the far lands beyond the tropic seas—the call of mountain and glen, islands and seas, hearth and home. You will be happy now to the end, because the waves that hushed you to sleep in your cradle will hush you to sleep when the last night falls. You have come back. But they will never return. Somewhere in far Rhodesia there is a Scot who has found a plant on the veldt whose root when burning smells like peat. He goes out to gather it, and throws it on the fire when his brother Scots arrive. But for you the peats lie round your door, and the blue reek rises daily like the fragrant incense of home.

There's a wee, wee glen in the Hielan's,
    Where I fain, fain would be ;
There's an auld kirk there on the hill-side
    I wearie sair to see.
In a low lythe nook in the graveyard
    Drearily stands alane,
Marking the last lair of a' I lo'ed,
    A wee moss-covered stane.

There's an auld hoose sits in a hollow
    Half-happit by a tree ;
At the door the untended lilac
    Still blossoms for the bee ;
But the auld roof is sairly seggit,
    There's nane now left to care ;
And the thatch ance sae neatly stobbit
    Has lang been scant and bare.

Aft as I lie 'neath a foreign sky
    In dreams I see them a'—
The auld dear kirk, the dear auld hame,
    The glen sae far awa'.
Dreams flee at dawn, and the tropic sun
    Nae ray o' hope can gie ;
I wander on o'er the desert lone,
    There's nae mair hame for me.

                                    CHARLES MURRAY.

SUTHERLAND

XXII

WANDERINGS IN SUTHERLAND

A CURE FOR WINTER WEARINESS

WITH the first dawn of April I made for the North.
The winter was past. A burst of bird music floated
in at the open window and wakened me. Like an
arrow from a bow I sped from crowds to solitude, and
ere nightfall I was wandering among the islands of the
Ness. The next day I gazed once more on the glorious
view up Strath Oykell from Invershin Station, and
within an hour was on the road that leads for fifty
miles through the wilds of Sutherland to the blue
waters of the West. That night I fell asleep to the
sound of waves breaking on the shore. But the wanderlust was on me, and I knew that there would be no
peace of mind until I stood looking out on the seas of
Wrath with the winds from the Arctic blowing about
me.

To every man his own thoughts of any land. As I
travelled over the hill road from Lairg to Rosehall, on
the Oykell river, Sutherland meant to me, that April
day, a sanctuary of solitude, a geological hammer, and
the Marquis of Montrose.

Montrose ! It was over this very road that the great

Marquis travelled south one April day in 1650, with a gather-up army of 1200 men to make his last stand at Carbisdale. Publicly disowned, but privately encouraged by his double-dealing master, Charles II, Montrose saw his little army surprised and cut to pieces by Strachan's cavalry. After the rout, and with several wounds on him, he wandered westward, disguised as a countryman, through the trackless desert for two days and nights without food. On the third day he ventured to beg some bread and milk at a herd's shieling. The hue and cry was soon out, and he was captured by one of the servants of Neil Macleod of Assynt. Assynt himself knew that the head of Montrose was worth enough gold to set up his impoverished family for good. So on 30th April he confined the Marquis in his dungeon at Ardvreck Castle, on the shores of Loch Assynt. The ruin on the road close by the Loch is Calda House, a mansion built by the Mackenzies in the seventeenth century; but yon stark wall on the spit of land is all that is left of Ardvreck. Scots memories are long, for here am I calling down a malediction on Neil Macleod of Assynt, and lifting my bonnet to the gallant Marquis. Be a man's sympathies with Covenanter or Cavalier, none will deny that Montrose was one of the greatest soldiers of history, and that it is a dastardly thing for any man to betray friend or enemy for the sake of money.

All the way up Strath Oykell to Loch Assynt I was thinking of Montrose and Neil Macleod, and of two poems. The one was by Ian Lom, the Highland bard :

> Neil's son of woeful Assynt,
>   If I in net could take thee,
> My sentence would condemn thee
>   Nor would I spare the gibbet.

> Stript tree of the false apples,
>   Without esteem or fame or grace ;
> Ever murdering each other,
>   Mid dregs of wounds and knives.

The other poem was by Montrose himself, and it is one of the purest lyrics ever written :

> My dear and only love, I pray,
>   That little world of thee
> Be governed by no other sway
>   Than purest monarchy.
>
> He either fears his fate too much
>   Or his deserts are small,
> That dares not put it to the touch
>   To win or lose it all.
>
> But if thou wilt prove faithful, then,
>   And constant to thy word,
> I'll make thee glorious by my pen
>   And famous by my sword.

O Neil Macleod ! What thought you and your lady wife of Lemlair when the body of that gallant cavalier was dismembered in Edinburgh, the limbs sent to the chief towns in Scotland, the head spiked on the Tolbooth, and the body buried beside the gallows on the Boroughmuir ?

> Death wrapping to thee, base one ;
>   Ill did thou sell the righteous,
> For the meal of Leith,
>   And two-thirds of it sour.

The wild west of Sutherland has given rise to many geological controversies. The floor of the whole region is laid on the oldest rocks in Great Britain—the Lewisian gneiss. My first view of Sutherland, long ago, was from the sea. Seen from a ship's deck, the whole land seems to rise out of the water in bare rounded domes of rugged rock, which tumble over each other like mountainous waves, as far as the eye can reach. Above this wilderness great mountain masses stand sentinel. Without a tree or bush to break the grassless monotony, these rounded bosses have been worn smooth by the ice, and huge blocks of rock—the debris of the glaciers—are poised on the very top of the dome-like hills. Such is the floor of Sutherland. But what of the mountains?

I climbed to a high top north of Scourie on a clear April day and saw the whole panorama of Sutherland and Ross. The giant mountains stood up from the rolling floor—Ben More Assynt, Glasven, Quinag, Canisp, Suilven, Cul Mhor, Cul Beg, with the outline of the Coigeach hills on the south. The long low point of Stoer stretched westwards into the Minch, and the Old Man of Stoer stood at the very nose of the promontory like a mighty sentry keeping watch. Some of these mountains, like Quinag, show three distinct groupings of rock—the primeval gneiss below; the horizontal bands of warm-coloured Torridon sandstone above; with white quartzite wreathing the summit. Seen from the sea, Suilven stands up like a precipitous sugar loaf. Ben Stack is a pointed pyramid of gneiss. Ben Clibrick is one imposing mass of schist. Ben Loyal, with its four pointed tops farther north, is a picturesque mountain of granite.

But the geological miracle of Sutherland is the extraordinary series of upthrusts of archaic gneiss, which have not only been forced from beneath thousands of feet of overlying strata, but have been pushed bodily over these strata, sometimes for a distance of at least

NORTH WEST SUTHERLAND

ten miles. These rocks have been heaved up, thrust over, and crushed together by the action of colossal natural forces.

Had a traveller only time enough, he could pick up a story in every place-name in the Highlands. For example, when I was warming myself at the fire in the little fishing inn at Altnacealgach, on Loch Borralan, I remembered that the very name, *Alt-na-cealgach*, meant the Burn of the Cheat. Here the county of Ross makes a strange wedge-like invasion northwards into Sutherland, as far as Conaveall and the slopes of Ben More Assynt. The truth is, that a dispute took place here long ago as to the boundaries of the two counties ; and when certain witnesses were called they maintained that while they were walking the boundaries they had never wandered a step off Ross-shire ground. Neither they had. But they had first filled their shoes with Balnagowan earth ! Hence, Alt-na-cealgach, the Burn of the Cheat.

The roads in the west are narrow and rough. Perhaps the worst road in Sutherland is that which runs over from Skiag Bridge, on the shores of Loch Assynt, to Kylesku. When I crossed it the day was heavenly. The serrated ridges of Quinag stood blazing against the sky, like a wall of the world. On the Kylesku side there is a hairpin bend a few miles above Unapool. At this bend two men were repairing the track. They had dug a long trench on one side of the road, and were filling it in with a series of heaps made up of great stones. As we approached they began to flatten out the heaps, that we might pass more comfortably over what would then be something like a river bed. The remaining part of the road was too narrow for any car. But while I was wondering how long it would take, the man at the wheel took my breath away by driving right over these miniature moraine heaps in the trench. Not a word was spoken, and we came through without a mishap. But I thought of the billiard-table roads of the south.

Another road in Sutherland provided a splendid thrill. On the east side of Loch Erriboll there is a nasty steep hill, with neither parapet nor fence on the seaward side, which falls away abruptly to the shore. At the top of this hill there is a rocky bluff round which the road turns suddenly, so that it is impossible at this dangerous corner to see what is beyond. We were creeping up the road and round this rock at the top, when, like a bolt from the blue and without a sound, a motor-bicycle whisked round the rock, on the wrong side of the road, scooted across the nose of the car, and by a miracle did not skid on the grass and so somersault down the slope to the sea. But somebody ought to have been killed.

All which things I deliberately record to indicate that Sutherland roads are very narrow, very rough, often dangerous, and that only fools rush on where angels hold their breath.

It was at Loch Culag that I sat with my back to the south side of a bracken bank and baked in the sun. On the north side of the bank a clean cold wind was blowing, above was a blue-white sky. In a little grey wood one warbler was dribbling out music for all the world. The loch below me rippled with laughter in the dazzling light. Beyond the tawny hills the weird sugar loaf of Suilven rose into the April sky with a sprinkle of snow picking out the paralleled rings round the summit.

To the north of Scourie lies the bird-haunted sanctuary of Handa Island. After a walk along the hill-tops I climbed down a little cliff opposite the island, and sat perched above the restless waves, betwixt the sky and sea. The great cliffs were in shadow ; a blue sea stretched away to the uttermost isles ; the churn of the tides broke in white spray at the foot of the cliffs and on the skerries ; Skye, Harris, and the Lews slept on the horizon, and the white-winged birds wheeled and cried about me. Here at last was solitude supreme, and it added to the peace to know that no one on the earth knew exactly where I was.

When I reached Durness I found a village asleep. The store was closed because the store-keeper was at the seed-sowing. The gaunt remains of an hotel stand at the cross-roads, gutted by fire. Nobody was within sight. But it seemed all the better because of the sense of peace that reigned.

At Rispond I hummed the melancholy " Rispond Family Elegy," and recalled Rob Donn's poem about the two miserly bachelor brothers who lived at Rispond, with their hoard of gold buried in the earth within sight of their windows. The breakers were making melancholy music on the sands between the rocks, but no dirge is half so sad as the miser's mistake, which turns this glorious world into a prison cell.

> No wrong had they to any done,
>   Judging by human ken ;
> But, neither had they helped in aught
>   Their needy fellow-men.

Then comes the long round of Loch Eriboll and the Kyle of Tongue. Tongue is a very pleasant place after having been in the wilds of Western Sutherland— a long, narrow kyle of shallow water, with endless stretches of sand when the tide recedes ; a bien-looking village with cultivated fields and woods along the shore, and the ruin of Castle Varrich crowning the little hill opposite. Only at Tongue did I realise that for ten days I had seldom seen any trees or wandered in any considerable woods. True, at Scourie you will find two palm trees growing in an old garden. But here the birds were singing in the deep-gladed woods, and the road was lined with thick-growing pine trees.

The wanderlust was now satisfied. I had shaken off all the winter weariness. The South was calling once more. So there was nothing for it but to take the long forty-mile trek to Lairg again, by Loch Loyal and Loch Naver. At Altnaharra Inn I loitered among memories of the happy long ago. In a little wood near Loch Shin I heard the whistle of a whaup. But what it meant to me none could ever guess.

> What thochts o' the lang grey moorlan'
>   Start up when I hear that cry!
> The times we lay on the heather brae
>   At the well, lang syne gane by.
>
> Yet—even yet—if I wander
>   Alane by the moorlan' hill,
> That queer wild cry frae the gurly sky
>   Can tirl my heart-strings still.
>
>   R. Wanlock Reid.

XXIII

THE WORSHIP STONES OF EDDRACHILLIS

A WILD TEMPLE

THERE is a lonely place on the shores of Sutherland which will always be a hallowed spot to me. It is one of those little inlets of the sea, or viks, which you will find all round the great Bay of Eddrachillis, and up the desolate coast by Laxford to Cape Wrath. Like the blessed life itself, holiday happiness demands wide views, plenty of sunlight, and a beauty of clouds which only adds to the wonder of this world as God has made it. Here, in Sutherland, all these boons are mine.

Sitting on the top of a grassy headland whose rock-face falls sheer to the sea for 200 feet, the short-sighted eyes of a city man might well be strained in trying to catch a glimpse of infinity. The sea is one vast plane of blue, from the Point of Stoer to the Butt of Lewis, round which the ships sail on and on until they come to the Arctic ice. Farther south the hills of Harris float on the rim of the ocean like the elusive lands of Tir-nan-og. Above these Hebrid Isles a long thin line of pearly cloud stretches from end to end of the summer world. A few miles up the Sutherland coast the nose of Handa is thrust into the sea, and yonder to the south the Old Man of Stoer, the eternal sentry of the island-studded Bay of Eddrachillis, stands at the very point of the long flat headland. Over this long black line of Stoer rise the giants of Assynt.

L

Far below me the sea is glittering in the sun with ripples of silvery laughter. The only sounds are the call of the seabirds, the bleating of sheep, the croak of a raven among the rocks, the grumble of the restless seas as they break everlastingly at the foot of the cliffs, and the whisper of the summer breeze. The beauty of such a day is a benediction, and peace is borne on the winds of God which blow straight from heaven.

O these northern days ! White wings flashing above the deep blue sea, green turf by the yellow sands, grey lichened rocks, and ruddy headlands washed by the restless tides, with peat reek drenching the soft airs that play about the crofts. Would that I could waft the wonder of it all across the world to every exiled Celt who swelters in a tropic clime or dreams of home on the barren veldt.

But there is something of great historic interest lying below the precipice at the head of the little vik. Standing on the high ground looking down into the vik you get another vista out to sea. The flat lands of Stoer, about Oldany and Clashnessie, cut across the picture from cliff to cliff, and in the glittering sea the isles of Eddrachillis are framed between the mighty rocks. Descending the steep path, the first thing that meets the eye is a great tumble of rocks which have fallen from the cliff and blocked the head of the vik. These form a mighty bulwark to the sea, and behind this heap of primeval débris, in a hollow surrounded by grassy braes, lie the Worship Stones. At first sight one might mistake this well-defined circular enclosure of stones for a sheep fank. But no ordinary shepherd would gather his sheep and lambs in such an inaccessible hollow at the head of a vik.

BEN LAOGHAL, TONGUE

No. This is one of the most interesting of modern ecclesiastical remains in the whole of the Scourie district. It is a veritable Bucht of God. For here, after the Disruption in 1843, when the newly-formed Free Church congregation of Eddrachillis could find no other place of worship, they built this solid wall of stones in the form of an oval shelter, and it became the foundation of their " tent in the wilderness," where they worshipped God, no man making them afraid.

You can still trace the steep winding path—all grass-grown now—which led down into the hollow. Step down it, and where it turns to the right at the bottom you will find an open doorway in the wall facing you. By this door all the worshippers would enter the Sanctuary. Right across the enclosure there is a second doorway in the farther wall, by which the preacher would enter to address the huddled flock of Christ. At the right-hand side of the preacher's door there stands a great flat natural outcrop of rock, which would doubtless serve for a raised pulpit.

What a perfect auditorium ! The whole congregation, when in the " tent," would be surrounded by a circle of grassy banks and shattered rocks, with a canopy of blue sky overhead. In quiet weather it must have been a very peaceful house of God—but, in a time of storm, the sound of many waters and great sea billows behind the fallen rocks must have well-nigh drowned the voice of the preacher or the voices of the worshippers as they sang :

> Though hills amid the seas be cast,
>   Though waters roaring make
> And troubled be, yea, though the hills
>   By swelling seas do shake.

The preacher, facing his audience, would see more than a mass of reverent faces. He would see the mighty cliff rising on the right and the huge rocks that had been cast down—literally the rock of ages which had been cleft from that terrific bastion of the world. But of the thundering sea there is not a glimpse, and, standing to-day on the preacher's rock, one might be far away from the restless waves, were it not that they are breaking within a stone's throw on the iron-bound shores.

I have never spoken in a sanctuary where the acoustics were more perfect. It might be the theatre of Dionysus at Athens, where you stand on the lowest level with tier upon tier of seats rising in circles on three sides. What a place for a conventicle!

As I measured the circular enclosure—39 feet by 27 feet—I remembered with joy that the old bitterness of Secession and Disruption in the land is all over, and that we have now seen a great reunion of Scots Presbyterianism. Shall these Worship Stones, then, mean nothing to us? Far from it. For, like every Covenanter's grave on a Lowland moor, they only make the history of this land all the more dear to a devout Scot. Wherever we find in these Highland wastes a cup-marked boulder, an old grey cross, a Norse place-name, or a Celtic old word, we know that we are the inheritors of a great past which no wise man can ever forget.

So I sit in the sun within this holy circlet of stones listening to the winds whispering among the rocks, to the sea-birds calling over the breakers, and to the old raven croaking far up among the craggy hills, and I hear the voices of the dead raised in a psalm, as they praise God for all His mercies. Then, as I climb down the rocks to the sea-cave close by, where the waves are booming eerily in its innermost recesses, I see an otter creeping stealthily up from the sea to his hidie-hole under a fallen boulder, his sleek body, narrow head, and long tapering tail all dripping with the salt water. So wild, so desolate, yet so sacred is this little vik to-day—for through the ruined walls of the Worship Stones the winds of memory will blow for ever.

XXIV

HIGHLAND RAIN

ON LAND AND SEA

MANY people have asked me why the sun always seems to be shining when I take my journeys up and down Scotland. For in this land of grey weather, where rain is our common heritage, and the average Scot is accustomed to be wet, there would seem to be something false about descriptions of scenery which is made beautiful by perpetual sunshine and seas that are always blue. Why, then, this constant sunshine ? Because I deliberately pick out the radiant days and believe that but for the rain the Western Highlands of Scotland would not be so famous all the world over for such wonderful colour effects on sea and land. So, like a true lover, I have a fine gift of forgetting when it comes to the dull, grey days.

Highland rain ! To a man who has spent part of every year of his life in some part of the Highlands of Scotland, rain of sheer necessity becomes a commonplace.

To-day, for example, in this little township of North-West Sutherland, we have been prisoners of hope for weeks on end. Despite a few brilliant blinks, rain has become a daily damper to our spirits. After the true Highland manner, the clouds have always been going to clear, and then they have closed in worse than ever. This morning they opened their vial of wrath, and the rain came crashing down on the glass veranda like a judgment. Never within a fairly long memory have I known Highland rain that was so persistent or so terrific. Our thoughts naturally turned to the Flood when, at eleven o'clock in the forenoon, the lamp had to be lit because of the darkness.

There are three orders of rain north of the Highland line. There is the soft, warm, persistent smirr which wraps the hills in mist and wets without injury those who plod on in a pother of clammy heat. There is also the sharp shower—heavy, enveloping, sudden—which makes a man fly for shelter to the nearest rock. But it goes as quickly as it comes, and then, when the sun blazes forth out of the bluest of skies, the hills literally gleam with beauty in the clear shining that comes after the rain. Lastly, there is the constant, never-ceasing, day-and-night downpour which generally lasts for three days, reduces the ardent lover of the open to a state of absolute despair, and fills the Highland kitchen with a whole wardrobe of soaking clothes, dripping stockings, and sodden shoes. For in this land of floods and fountains, the coat has not yet been invented which can be called waterproof.

The soft smirr, the sudden shower, the persistent downpour—these are the three kinds of Highland rain to which those who sail the Western seas and climb the Northern hills have been long accustomed. An artist known to me, whose home is on a Western isle, makes an invariable practice of boring holes in the soles of every pair of new shoes he buys, that the rain may have an easy and immediate exit, and when he sets off for a tramp or a climb, he usually walks through the first burn. In all this there is much wisdom. For the man who is always trying to avoid puddles can know nothing of the joys of travel; whereas, there is instant peace of mind for all who accept the inevitable and realise that there need be nothing injurious in getting wet.

It is almost unbelievable how suddenly a Highland stream can come down when there has been a cloud-burst on the hills. A man may be walking quietly by a burn-side, casting a line, and almost before he is aware a cloudburst far up the mountainside may send down a wall of water which will sweep him off his feet. One such cloudburst took place at the Burn of the Cheat, close by the Inn of Altnacealgach, many years ago. The day had been intensely hot. At four o'clock in the afternoon a fisher sat on a stone in the dried-up bed of the stream to cool his hands and feet. The air was electric, and a peal of thunder came from the copper-coloured clouds on the hill-top. Then black darkness set in; the storm burst; and rain fell in torrents. The burn, which had been almost dry half an hour before, was now a foaming flood. The stone conduit could not hold it, so it spread far and wide over the road and several acres of fields. Stones were hurled down the hill-side with terrific poundings. A calf standing in the byre was half drowned. The fisherman dropped his kilt, a woman servant and a girl of fifteen took off their shoes and stockings, and all three plunged through the flood to rescue the young bull which was standing in three feet of water. One pushed him with a pole, while another lassoed him with a rope, and so rescued the terrified beast. Sandy, the landlord's brother, had just waded on to the bridge when the whole arch broke down and he was sent swirling down among the debris to the lochside, where he only saved himself by clinging to the bank. The flood subsided as quickly as it came, and yet not a drop of rain had fallen three miles away.

Sandy's legs were sorely crushed by his accident. So next morning a shepherd who was well known for his surgical abilities called at the inn for a dram. He was asked to operate on the sufferer, and immediately the theatre was prepared. Sandy was set down on a kitchen chair, with his cutty pipe in his mouth, and each bared leg stretched across a pail of hot water. The shepherd searched among the bruises for a vein near the ankle and inserted his rude lancet with a vigorous push which brought a Gaelic yell out of poor Sandy. The patient, however, quietly replaced his pipe and tholed the next jag more philosophically, after which both surgeon and subject pledged each other over a gill of whisky.

But rain on sea is even more terrible than rain on land, and I can recollect one or two wild rainstorms on the Western seas.

The first was on Loch Fyne. The squall was heralded by a blue-black line of hissing water that came nearer and nearer with relentless speed. The order was given to take in the big jib and hoist the storm jib on the little twelve-tonner. Before the process was completed, however, the squall was on us. The rain literally lashed the face so hard that the eyes were blinded and the fumbling hands failed at first to slip the cleat of the sheets into the iron eyelet of the jib, which was flapping in the gale like a thing bewitched. Then followed a clout on the side of the head with the iron eyelet, but it was all part of the day's work, and the job had to be done. At last the jib was secured, the sheet was hauled taut, and the boat staggered on through the plunging seas.

Again, it was in the open water between Rhum and
Skye. A strong sea was running, and the old schooner
was thrashing into the storm under shortened sail.
With a long leg and a short one we were attempting
to beat round the Point of Sleat. The rain never ceased.
Great seas churned past us. For eight hours we were
beating against wind and wave. One cap after another
went overboard. The lee deck was all awash, and the
streaming whips of heaven lashed us without mercy
until we were like drowned rats. When evening came,
we were forced to give in, so we put about and ran
back with a following wind to the anchorage in Loch
Scresort, from which we had set out in the morning.

And yet there are always compensations. That is
the blessed adventure of bad weather—you never know
what a shower is going to bring you, and I have made
some fine friendships while sheltering from the rain.

On a cerain road in Skye I was caught in one of
those tremendous showers which are brewed among
the Coolins, and then pour their largess over the lower
lands. There was neither rock nor cottage near-by, so
when the deluge came I made for a tinkers' camp which
I knew was snugly pitched beside a brawling stream.
The day before I had made the acquaintance of the
tinkers and guessed that they were Ullapool men,
because they advertised their domicile by the large
letters U.L. which were painted on the old brown
sail that made their bee-hive tent. In every tinkers'
camp in the Highlands you will find an old set of bagpipes, and the sure way to the heart of a piping mugger
is to give him a set of old pipe reeds. A little collection
of these I carry with me, as a kind of visiting-card in
the remote Highlands, for my nomad friends. Having
presented a set to one of the Ullapool lads the day

before, when he was piping in the village, I knew I was sure of a welcome in the long brown tent when the clouds burst. So I dived into the tent, streaming with rain, and was soon steaming before a roaring stove that made an atmosphere which would have suffocated any but the most robust. How long I sat I know not—for the *ceilidh* was good.

This is the twenty-second day on which we have had heavy rain in Scourie. Here, then, is the conclusion of the whole matter which an illustrious Highlander has for ever immortalised in verse :

> But, if you're a delicate man
>   And of wetting your skin are shy,
> I'd have you know before you go,
>   You'd better not think of Skye.

XXV

HAUNTS OF THE VIKINGS

ROUND THE SHORES OF SUTHERLAND

SITTING alone on this wild headland in the far North, munching bread and cheese, with my bundle lying on the turf beside me, I am watching the restless sea grumbling at the foot of the cliffs which stand like eternal walls on either side of the creek. At any moment a high-prowed ship full of fair-haired Vikings might appear, for in this lone land there is nothing visible at the moment to tell whether you are in the ninth century or the twentieth—no house, no road, no living creature ; only the limitless ocean, a few desolate and uninhabited islands, and the white birds flashing above the waves.

I wonder how many Scotsmen realise that for 400 years—from 800 to 1263—the whole of North-West Scotland was ruled by the Norsemen—those consummate sea-rovers who knew every creek or vik on the islands and mainland. They were called Vikings, or Creekmen, because they haunted these viks or inlets of the sea. They conquered the original Pictish inhabitants of the country—although I tremble to discuss who the Picts were—and after four centuries the hardy Norsemen left behind them strange place-names which you will find scattered over the whole of this Sudhr-land, from Oykel to Wrath. For, wherever you come across a Bol, a Vik, a Ness, a Stac, a Cleit, a Geo, a Sgeir, a Tunga, a Dal, a Fjord, a Gil, a Setr an Ob, or a Smoo, there you can be sure that a Viking lived.

Not so many years ago the body of a Viking, a thousand years old, was found encased in ice within the Arctic Circle. Preserved from head to heel, more perfectly than an Egyptian mummy, the body of this Viking, standing upright in a huge iceberg which was cast up on the east coast of Greenland, was discovered by some Danish doctors. Seven feet in height, clad in ancient armour, gripping a spear and shield, the head crowned with the winged helmet of Norse Royalty, the whole figure was dimly visible through the transparent tomb of ice. When the ice was chipped away the Viking looked as if he had died but yesterday; the hair and moustache long and red and silky; and the body neither shrunken nor dried up in any way. This wonderful specimen of a Royal Rover was taken to Copenhagen, and the question was immediately asked —Was this the body of Eric the Red, who was famed in saga and rune as a fearless voyager ? For many historians believe that Eric the Red landed on the shores of North America 400 years before Columbus sailed on the little *Santa Maria*. It was this same Viking, Eric the Red, who discovered Greenland (A.D. 985), and as the *Eyrbyggja Saga* tells us, " he called the land which he had found *Greenland*, for he said it would make men's minds long to go there if it had a fine name."

There are five great fjords on the north-east coast of Sutherland, every one of which bears to-day a purely Norse name—Laxford, Inchard, Durness, Erriboll, and Tongue. Of all the five, the wildest are Loch Laxford and Loch Inchard—long deep arms of the sea running into the barren Lewisian gneiss.

How wisely these old Vikings bestowed their place-names ! They called the first fjord *Lax-fjord*, that is Salmon-Loch, because they found it full of salmon. And after a thousand years it remains true to its name, for the little Laxford river is perhaps the finest salmon river in the north, and fish are still taken out of it up to a weight of over 40 pounds.

Inchard was the *Engi-fjord*, or Meadow Loch, of the Norsemen. Durness was their *Deer's-Point*. Erriboll was their *Eyrr-bol*, or Beach-Town. Tongue was their *Tunga*, a Tongue of Land.

As I wandered from one clachan to another along the shores of Laxford, right out to the seaboard opposite to the Isle of Handa, I wondered how the half-dozen families in each place found a living. But the sea is full of fish, their little crofts are smiling green in the sun, and doubtless these hardy Northmen of to-day pity us far more than we town folks pity them. Foindlemore, Fanigmore, and Tarbet—these are the happy townlands of many a Celt, both young and old. And for intelligence ? Of the two strong lads who rowed me from Tarbet out to Handa, the younger, who was only in his 'teens, used geological terminology in a way that would have put most city lads to shame.

The road to Kinloch Bervie also runs high above Loch Inchard, from one prosperous township to another. From the point where the road rises to a height of nearly 300 feet there are glorious views across the Sutherland wilderness. On the south side of the loch a wild high path leads from Rhiconich to Rhimichie. Indeed, so foreign-sounding are the names of the clachans about Loch Inchard that you might be travelling in another land, and if you ever reach Sheigra, on the Atlantic coast, you may safely say you have come to the end of all things where the only outlook is to infinity.

BALNAKEILL CHURCH, DURNESS

Returning to Rhiconich, the road leads north to Durness, with wide prospects to Arkle, Foinnaven, and Spionnaidh. Then the wild rocks of Western Sutherland are left behind, and when you have passed Gualin, which means a " shoulder "—the real summit of the glen—you descend to Keoldale Ferry, where you cross the Kyle of Durness for Cape Wrath. You are now in a region of flat sheep lands, green fields, wide waters, and homely hills—the whole reason for this remarkable change of scenery being that you have left the archaic gneiss, and are now in a region of limestone. The ruins of the Pictish towers which line this strath remind you of the ancient inhabitants of the land, who must have greatly resented the invasion of the Vikings.

It was with longing eyes I looked across at Keoldale to the road which leads to Wrath. The Norsemen never bestowed a name with more exactitude when they called that uttermost cliff of Sutherland *Hvarf*—the Turning Point. For in all their voyages from Scandinavia to the Western Isles these sea-robbers would be glad to turn southwards to the sunny seas when they came to the beetling cliffs of Wrath. Once round Wrath, the Turning Point, and they would be delivered from the treacherous tides and storms of the Pettland or Pictland Firth, which we call Pentland now.

The village of Durness, or the Deer's Point, is an unspoiled clachan. The first time I visited Durness I was a victim of speed. But on this day of sunlit glories I turned westward past the ruined hotel, and came to the place of pilgrimage for all who love the poetry of the Celt, about a mile from the village. It is the church-yard of Balnakeill, where Rob Donn, the celebrated poet of the Reay country, is buried.

I shall treasure to the end of my life my first vision

of Balnakeill Bay—an immense sweep of white sand
over which the waves were rippling in long green
curves, blue waters sparkling in the sun, with an outlook to the Great North Sea between Geo Dubh and
Far Out Head—so wide and wonderful, and so far
from the madding crowd !

At the head of this beautiful bay stands the old
churchyard of Durness with its roofless church, and
close by it the bald mansion-house of Balnakeill, which
was once the residence of the Bishops of Caithness,
who came to hunt on the Deer's Ness, and the residence
at a later date of the noble family of Reay. This church
was built in 1619 on the site of an older one which was
attached to Dornoch Monastery. Doubtless long before
that date there was a still older cell of the Celtic Church
on this spot. The ruined walls and the crow-stepped
gables are all ivy-covered now, and inside may be seen
an old circular font and an ancient tomb with this
quaint inscription :

> Donald Macmurchov hier lyis lo.
> Vas il to his freind var to his fo :
> Trve to his maister in veird and vo. 1623.

In this churchyard stands a memorial to Rob Donn,
before which all lovers of Celtic literature will uncover
the head. For here was a natural genius who, despite
the fact that he could neither read nor write, composed
Celtic poems and melodies which were kept alive by
tradition, and handed down by word of mouth from
one generation to another.

He was born at Altnacaillich, in Strathmore, at the
foot of Ben Hope, near the ruined tower of Dornadilla.
What a human combine was Rob Donn ! He was
literally cradled in song, for from his mother he inherited

the gift of poetry. As a boy he was most precocious, and had a wonderful power of repartee. Janet Mackay, whom he afterwards married, had a musical ear and a beautiful voice. Although Rob Donn was not " out " in the 'Forty-Five, he was a Jacobite poet, and wrote two political songs—one in praise of Prince Charlie, and the other on the shame of the Act which forbade the wearing of the Highland dress. He was a notorious killer of deer, a fine shot, and an unrepentant poacher. Indeed, on one occasion, when he was actually going to the Court to be tried for slaying deer, he saw a herd by the roadside, and to the consternation of his wife could not resist from shooting two of them.

" Go home," said he to her, " and if I do not return there will be all the more for you."

His gun was so dear to him that when he was growing too old for the hill he filled the barrel with deer tallow, climbed to the top of Ben Spionnaidh, took farewell of his beloved weapon, and buried it among the summit rocks of Carn-an-righ, that no other hand should ever touch it.

O Rob Donn! How well some of us understand you. I often wonder if the gun will ever be found ; for Rob Donn died in 1778, at the age of sixty-four ; and older weapons of the 'Forty-Five have been found among the rocks. Yet this poacher poet was such a clean-living man that he sang the praises of religion, and was appointed Assessor of Session in his native parish.

His poetry reflects the social life of his time in songs of the shieling, the harvest, the wool-waulking, and the drove road. He looked on nature with a seeing eye. His dirges are full of tears. His love songs are pure and tender. He abhorred insincerity, and his satires cut like a razor dipped in oil. For many years after

M

Rob Donn's death the only library in which his poems were to be found was the memory of his own people. But in the year 1829 the first edition of his poems was printed, and this handsome monument was erected over his grave by his fellow-countrymen.

All the way to Tongue the Norseman contends with the Celt in the place-names of this spacious land. The Smoo Cave, which Sir Walter gazed at in wonder, lies at the head of a little cove about a mile from Durness ; and it was well named *Smjuga* by the sea-rovers, for the name means a narrow cleft to creep through. A mile or two farther on, at a steep turn of the road, you look down on a bay of gleaming sand, and right across the wide waters of Erriboll to far-off Whitten Head—a white towering cliff which is a landmark to sailors. The Vikings called it *Hvitr*, the White Headland ; and the Celts called it *Kennagall*, the Headland of the Stranger —both true. For that cliff will always remain a gleaming cliff ; and to the very last day of the Norse occupation, when Haco, defeated at Largs, sailed for the last time round Whitten Head, it was called *Kennagall*, the Headland of the Stranger, by the Celts.

Loch Erriboll is one of the finest harbours in Britain. In this beautiful fjord of clear, deep water a whole fleet could anchor and ride out a gale in perfect safety. When you have circled its shores or taken the shorter way across its calm waters by Heilim Ferry it is but a mile or two over the heather to Loch Hope.

Surely the view from Hope Lodge up the loch to Ben Hope is one of the very finest in Sutherland ! And if you follow the road up the east side of Loch Hope for ten miles you will come to Altnacaillich, Rob Donn's birthplace, and to the finest of all the ruined towers in Sutherland, the Dun of Dornadilla. Here, long ago, a native king of that name lived. When Haco's ships were anchored in Loch Erriboll, the Norsemen landed to plunder the country-side. But a band of native warriors who were led by an officer of King Dornadilla surprised the raiders, and killed most of the strangers. Among the slain was the Norse commander, whose name was Urradal, and Strath Urradale bears his name to-day. That was the last of the strangers.

All that is a tale a thousand years old. But still we see as in a dream these fair-haired strangers in the blue-eyed, flaxen-headed children of tempest who travel south or cross the storm-tossed Minch from the Outer Isles to seek their fortunes in the cities of the world to-day.

Some time ago a print appeared in *The Scotsman* of a modern Viking ship—the Raold Amundsen—moored in the Thames opposite the Houses of Parliament. Every one who stepped aboard that perfect repro-duction of a Norse galley was stepping across ten centuries of history. For we are still a seafaring folk, and the hardy Vikings whose blood flows in our veins must look with prideful eyes from their Valhalla on the monster ships that are launched from our yards. They knew the wonders of the deep, and their sagas are full of poetry. To them the sea was The Glittering Home. The sky was The Wind Weaver. The wind itself was The Never Silent. The very rocks were The Bones of the Sea. The rain was The Tears of the Clouds, and they called the clouds The Wind Floating. In life the Viking loved his long boat, and after death he was sometimes buried in his ship. Little wonder that his last words were :

I will go down
To the steeds of the sea.

XXVI

THE ISLAND OF HANDA

A BIRD SANCTUARY

My heart went out to Scourie when I came down the hill one April evening and took in at a glance this little unspoiled Sutherland township.

A scatter of white houses; crofts on the green hill above the sea; a tiny church, an old lodge among trees, a little bay looking to the sunset, a circlet of white sand with a lonely place of graves above; the nose of Handa Island making a perpetual rampart on the north-west; one or two skerries, a restless sea, now sparkling bright as an emerald, now cold and grey, but for ever grumbling round the rocks—that is Scourie.

To watch the sunlight flashing over the Minch between Sutherland and Lewis, or the rain-swept seas lashing white round those desolate islands and skerries which have names on a map but no living inhabitants except the sea-birds and the whiskered mild-eyed seals; no sail on the horizon; no summer visitors as yet on the mainland to spoil the unbroken life of the crofting townships, or to bring the breath of a fremmit world into these utter desolations—this is to enjoy the blessing of the separate.

There is always something fascinating about an island, especially if it lies in the lap of the Western seas

LOCH STACK, SUTHERLAND

and floats in the sunset. To live at Scourie is to be always looking out to Handa—from the hills, from the shores, from the fishing banks. It keeps pulling at your heart, until at last you have to take a boat and go out across the sea to explore the mysteries of this lonely island with the wild cliffs.

The first time I visited Handa we sailed out from Scourie on a heavenly day, which had cleared up after a depressing morning of rain. It was in that never-to-be-forgotten August of the thirty days' rain. But the half-dozen days that had sun blinks in them were all the brighter when they did come. The waves rolled in from the Atlantic in long tumbling masses of blue water, and when we got to the outside of the island and were sailing under the beetling cliffs, which rise straight up from the sea like built walls of Old Red Sandstone, the boat was sometimes hidden in the trough of the ocean, and sometimes racing on the crest of a great billow. With a wind blowing fresh from the west, the whole sea was one tumbling mass of restless indigo. On such a day the heart of a sailor sings with joy. All the time we were watching the waves breaking at the foot of the rocky walls. Clouds of white spray searched the red cliffs like showers of snow, while the white birds screamed and whirled with delight along the face of the precipices, like little bits of flashing life in the brilliant blue-white world.

When we came to the Stack of Handa, which is a great mass of isolated rock separated from the main cliff on the north side of the island, the sea began to moderate, and when we sailed into the Sound we were in a region of sheltered waters, with the sun blazing down on the barren shores of Sutherland and on the white sands of Handa.

M 2

The island is low and almost flat on the eastern side, rising gradually in heathery moors to a height of 406 feet at the cairn on Sithean Mor above the cliffs on the western side. The reason for this is that the whole island is composed of stratified Torridon sandstone, which has been tilted up from the east and south-east to the west and north-west. It is about a mile and a half long by a mile across. One traveller writing on Handa says that " the Laurentian cliffs of Handa rise in sheer precipices 600 feet above the western sea." But the cliffs are not quite 400 feet high.

The next time I visited Handa I crossed in a rowing boat from the little clachan of Tarbet. This is an ideal excursion, for, if necessary, you can motor to Clashfern, on the Scourie-Durness road, or even to Foindlemore, walk to Tarbet, row out to the island, and after spending some hours there row all the way back to Scourie.

But whichever way you go to Handa you will find the sea alive with cormorants, terns, guillemots, razor-bills, puffins, and gulls. In the earlier months of the summer you will find the ledges of the cliffs alive with nesting birds. But in August the breeding-places are almost deserted. The stench of places like Ailsa Craig, the Bass Rock, and Handa is anything but pleasant, as those who have visited those bird sanctuaries know well. But that is only at the breeding-time.

The great blue-black cormorants stand motionless in little groups on the rocks, very solemn and sentinel-like, as if they were black-coated monks contemplating the mysteries of the deep. Or they fly at enormous speed across the water, with their long black necks stretched out in a straight line. Another name for the cormorants is St Cuthbert's Fowls, for they were the favourite birds of St Cuthbert (d. 687), who lived on Holy Island, off the coast of Northumberland, in the seventh century. That is why the priceless Lindisfarne Gospels have countless cormorants worked into the designs of the illumined pages. These Gospels were inscribed on the Holy Isle of Lindisfarne by Bishop Eadfrith about the year 700, " in honour of God and St Cuthbert," and after 1200 years they remain to-day in an almost immaculate condition within the British Museum. On one page alone there are eighty-eight cormorants worked into the beautiful design. So I never see a cormorant, or skart, winging its way across the stormy sea or standing motionless on a rock but I remember good St Cuthbert, who first saw the vision of Christ in a sheepfold of Lauderdale, and afterwards served God as a missionary to the wild inhabitants of the borders, both at Melrose and on the sea-girt isle of Lindisfarne.

The sands of Handa are white, and the machair above them stretches like an emerald carpet along the shore. At the north end of the machair you will find a sheepfold, a row of ruined foundations, and a tiny graveyard close by. There are only a few upright stones in the graveyard, with one flat table slab on which is carved the name of " Peter Morrison." Farther on there is a solitary shepherd's house without a tenant. That is Handa to-day—a group of ruined shielings, a handful of graves, two hundred shepherdless sheep, a bastion of terrific cliffs all splashed with the lime of sea-fowl, gleaming sands on the eastward shores, and the never-ending music of salt sea winds that blow from the lone Atlantic.

And yet there was once a Queen of Handa. In the early years of the nineteenth century there were about a dozen families on the island. They maintained themselves on fish and by taking the eggs of the sea-birds.

The men were fearless cragsmen, and swung each other over the cliffs on ropes. The oldest widow was always called the Queen of Handa, and she was acknowledged not only on the island but on the mainland as well. Emigration, however, or some other reason, swept the people from Handa, and to-day it is uninhabited.

Charles St John, who wrote his famous " Tour in Sutherland " in the year 1848, describes a somewhat pathetic experience. On approaching Handa he saw a large white cat sitting on the rocks looking wistfully towards the mainland. He also speaks of two shiploads of emigrants on the point of leaving a harbour near Scourie. Handa must have been deserted about that time ; the white cat probably being the stray pet of some of these emigrants, for " all the emigrants had left the island early in the spring for America." So Handa has been a no-man's land ever since the year 1848.

" She is waiting for the ferry," remarked the boat-man as they looked at the white cat. But—the ferry never came !

During the nesting season every ledge on the cliffs is crowded with birds. Guillemots stand in long lines wherever there is a footing place, competing with their second cousins the razorbills. Countless puffins hide in the holes at the top of the giddy heights. Clouds of birds fly about the face of the precipices and fill the air with the din of their calling. Indeed, so crowded are they in their flight that one might think a heavy snow shower had swept across the seas. It is at once a very beautiful and an awesome sight to stand there and gaze down at those fearsome cliffs, with clouds of screaming birds about you, and the waves churning themselves into yeasty foam on the deathly rocks far below. What a perfect bird sanctuary is this uninhabited island in the far North, with its unscaleable cliffs looking across the infinite seas to the far-off Arctic ice !

And yet to me scenery is always enhanced by human recollections. So I cannot forget the happy company that gathered on the machair above the pure white sands ; the blue-green waters all shot with sunlight that made a bath of perfect buoyancy for the long leisurely swim ; the blazing fire against the grey rock, where the kettles sang, and our hunger was more than satisfied ; the long lazy rest in the sun when the peace pipe was lit ; and, when it was nearly time to go, the shrill skirl of the bagpipe as a wild reel was danced by young and old on the fine close-cropt turf.

It is thus that the happy summer days spent by the sea, among the hills, or in the heathery pine woods beside a running stream, can never be wholly lost to us, when the dark days of winter imprison us in fog-bound streets, or compel some old campaigner to lie abed and suffer the pains of disablement, with many a misty dream of the open road and the steep ascent.

Did we brood on our sorrow
    And see all the future in strife,
Who would wait for the morrow,
    Or bear with the bleakness of life ?

'Tis only the setting
    Of sorrow that lets us live on :
The grace of forgetting
    All else but the joy that is gone ;

In the scenes we remember
    From months or from years that are by,
The fogs of December
    Gleam gold with the sun of July.

                GEOFFREY WINTHROP YOUNG.

XXVII

THE UNSEEN HOST

AND THE HOUSE OF HOSPITALITY

I DO not understand the man who finds time hanging heavily on his hand, who thinks life dull, or who has a constant quarrel with other people. The road teaches us many lessons, and if we do not learn them the fault is ours. To a wandering man who has eyes in his head, love in his heart, and a dash of humour, time flies, the world is teeming with interest, there is some good in everybody, and the house with the open door is never hard to find.

But there is this in travel for all who take the road —an added element of surprise. You set out every morning on an unknown adventure. The unexpected leaps out on you at every corner. You cease to anticipate to-morrow's programme, for beyond the sunset lies the unknowable. You take the road as it comes—thankfully, expectantly, without worry. You cease to harass yourself even about stopping-places. The world becomes a friendly place. All classes get levelled out. East End and West End mean nothing to those who have to trudge along the dusty path in the heat with all their belongings on their backs. So the tramp can teach the millionaire a great lesson in faith, for while he takes every man as he finds him, he takes no anxious thought for the morrow.

I have had many strange adventures on the road, but until that day in June I never had the mystical

experience of being entertained by an Unseen Host in
the heart of the Highlands.

I remember a haunting passage in " John Splendid,"
which describes seven broken men who were flying from
the black battle of Inverlochy. One inclement night
they stumbled on the empty house of Dalness in Glen
Etive, open to the night, with candles lit in the sconces,
a wood fire burning in the tapestry-hung hall, an untouched meal laid on the table, and bottles that winked
to the flicker of candle and hearth. An uncanny sight
for men that were hunted, desperate with hunger, and
apprehensive of being dirked at every road end. From
the open door and a multitude of little windows light
gushed lemon yellow on the lawn. Here was a house of
mystery, lit from tolbooth to garret, peat fires banked
high, and a fine supper waiting for any gangrel who
might step out of the inclement night into comfortable
hospitality. So, after some swithering and recon-
noitring, the seven men sat down to the feast, and
soon their tongues were loosened by generous draughts
of wine. Then they boldly threw their glasses on the
hearth, shuttered the windows to the lashing storm, and
hoped with a certain gaiety that there was no ambuscade.
But it was all a trap laid by the Macdonalds for this
handful of MacCailein's men. So the ploy ended with
dirks and a flight through the storm.

Not so with us. So far from being broken men, we
were four boon brothers housed in a hostelry at Inverness, with the river sparkling in the sun every morning
before the open door, and a witching view of the castle
turrets bathed in the midnight afterglow.

No man of any historic sense can travel up and down
the Great Glen, from Fort-William to Inverness, without
many thoughts of battle days. But the twentieth century

is not the seventeenth or the eighteenth, and we have now substituted the broad highway for Wade's old roads, the motor-car for the lumbering coach, the wireless for the local runner, and the telephone for the franked epistle. Time and space have been annihilated, and all the world knows to-day what is going on in the obscurest corner.

Yet the finest sensibilities are still untouched, and the mysteries have only been deepened. Far away in England a voice began to speak. Here, in the North, another answered. Again and again the voices spoke —one in Cheshire, one in Lochaber, and one in Inverness. The invisible speaker in Cheshire, whom we had never seen, was to become our unseen host. Only a *taibhsear* who has the gift of second sight could possibly gauge the degree of mystery that lies in those voices which are passing each other with soundless messages on the hundred thousand winds of the world, like phantom ships in a silent night.

That day we had travelled eleven miles on the old Wade Road, and fished Loch Duntalchaig from morning till night. When this road was opened in the year 1726 Lord Townsend and one or two other nobles drove over it in a great lumbering coach-and-six, to the astonishment of the natives, who had never seen a carriage on wheels. The Highlanders made deep obeisance to the gorgeous coachman, but paid no attention to the gentry inside. Indeed, the year before that, an old beldame with a wrinkled face saw the soldiers preparing to move a huge boulder.

"Fools!" she cried, "that stone will be there for ever!"

But when the stone began to move she gave forth an eldritch yell, and ran from the workmen, whom she took for warlocks.

AN TEALLACH: TOLL AN LOCHAIN

To-day the rumour goes that on the new North Road the ghost of General Wade has been seen wandering about on the still nights, silently examining the gradients and the bridges. But when the wraith stands at the bridges and thinks of his own, he sighs in the summer night for a beauty that is gone. The sighs are heard mostly in the region of Tomatin.

The next day dawned with all the heat and beauty of perfect midsummer. It was over fifty miles to the house of hospitality. But one hundred miles to-day is like an evening stroll to a man with a swift car. I will not linger on the legends by the way. But a man cannot pass by Castle Urquhart without thinking of De Bois and his lady wife keening on the eagle's crag. At Invermoriston the thoughts fly to the eight men who guarded Prince Charlie in the Cave at Corriegoe, and to Mackenzie's Cairn. At old Kilcummin many a poor Jacobite languished in the fort. Would that the grey ruin of Glengarry did not remind us of Pickle the Spy; or Tober-nan-ceann of the seven bloody heads washed in the well. But the moment we enter Lochaber our hearts go out to the gentle Lochiel and Dr Archie Cameron, who lost all for the Prince they would neither betray nor desert. Montrose, Argyle, Prince Charlie, and many a Scots king before them—did ever a high road take us through more history and heart-breaking romance than that which runs from Culloden to Inverlochy? Every foot of it cries out

> Of old, unhappy, far-off things,
> And battles long ago.

We arrived at noon, turned down a long avenue, and found the door of a great house standing wide open to the blazing sunshine, with all the west windows winking across to Lochiel's sanctuary at Achnacarry. Here, at this earthly paradise, the boon brothers arrived, as did the seven broken men at Dalness long ago, and found the open door, open windows, a feast spread on the table with the choicest of food, the best of drinks, and tobacco to suit all tastes.

But there was no sign of the host ! Yet for us the house was haunted.

Boats rode at the jetty ready for us to step aboard. From room to room we wandered at will. But there was no one in any of them. Empty, luxurious, quiet, soundless, their windows looked on one of the most romantic views in the Highlands. Yonder lay the Dark Mile, that *Mile Dorcha*, which is now no longer dark. Outby, the azaleas made a blaze of colour like a fire, and scented the warm airs most deliciously. But while there was the best of service at the table and Donald at the jetty to do our bidding with the boats and rods, there was no host to be seen anywhere. It was an eerie meal, with many a glance thrown over the shoulder to catch a glimpse of someone who never came.

The long afternoon was spent on the loch fishing for trout that were all asleep. The summer beauty was so hypnotic that it was hard to do anything but dream. The wind fell away, and the wonder of the woods and hills was mirrored in the sea of glass. The romance of the old days and the pathos of the lost cause so gripped our hearts that there was only one way of expressing it. So the gardener's pipes were borrowed, and after a little coaxing the bag was under the oxter, the ear was leaning fondly to the drones, and the whole pageant of history soon was rolling down the loch, waking the echoes of the dead, with " Lochiel's Gathering " for the march of the Cameron men to

Glenfinnan, and " Lochaber no More " for the name-
less men who died in exile, or among these hills where
Butcher Cumberland hunted the remnant like vermin.

It was quite inevitable that two men should land on
the shores of Achnacarry and wander for a little while
in the old haunts of Charlie and his friends. But there
comes a moment when the bravest mood is over, and
the heart ceases to feel. So as the white boat carried
us back swiftly again to the other shore in the radiant
light of the fading day a new port was put on the pipes,
and we drew in to the jetty with a perfect riot of Gaelic
gaiety. Then the world seemed emptied of all sound when
the chanter fell silent and the ribbons fluttered no more.

That evening Nature seemed to be swooning in a
dream of peace as we made our way up the shores of
the three lochs. When the stars came out the whole
day became a parable of that road which is more
mystical than any highway the feet of man has ever
travelled. Throughout this day of haunting happiness
we had been looking for a face that we had never seen,
and listening for a voice that we had never heard in the
flesh. Yet with what rare delight had our host been
entertaining us in his house of hospitality.

Little wonder, then, that to those of us who look on
this homely earth as a house of daily delights, and have
long ago realised that we are being entertained with a
Hospitality that is far beyond our deserts, these words
became the epilogue of a perfect day and lulled us to
sleep by the side of the running waters :

> Strange the world about me lies,
>   Never yet familiar grown—
> Still disturbs me with surprise,
>   Haunts me like a face unknown.
>   WILLIAM WATSON.

XXVIII

THE TEN COMMANDMENTS OF WALKING

A TRAMPER'S DECALOGUE

THE greatest pleasures are always the simplest, and the finest relaxations of man are to be enjoyed only by those who are content to return to the most primitive methods of travel. Riding a horse, sailing a boat, walking along the surface of this most wonderful world. Be a man as rich as Crœsus or as poor as Lazarus, nothing will ever take the place of these particular forms of open-air recreation.

But in this age of hurry I fear that walking—the slowest of all the methods of travel—requires some recommendation. Let me, therefore, state the Ten Commandments of Walking, for all who are about to throw the rucksack over their shoulders and set out for a tramping holiday on the summer roads.

The First Commandment is—THOU SHALT WALK, IF THOU WOULDEST KEEP WELL.

Walking is the healthiest exercise in the world. Let a man be ever so strong, there is no hope for his body unless he takes plenty of exercise in the open air. Walking is the best of all physical economies. It clarifies the mind, and exhilarates the spirit, just because it keeps every organ in the body working in a normal state of health. Thought and feeling are

192

largely determined by the physical condition of the man who thinks and feels. For all, therefore, who would come home from a holiday fit for work, happy-hearted, and mentally alert, this is the First Commandment—Thou shalt walk.

The Second Commandment is—THOU SHALT SET OUT PROPERLY EQUIPPED.

Travel light. Let your shoes be stout old friends. Eat little while you are tramping, drink less, and have no fear of the sun, the rain, the wind, or the weather. Carry everything on your back, in a rucksack that is properly slung, and in the hand nothing but a stick to swing rhythmically to your whistling or your songs, or to strike at a pebble or a dog, if you are attracted to the one or attacked by the other. And for clothes—let them also be like true friends, old, comfortable, weather-beaten.

The Third Commandment is—THOU SHALT HAVE NO PROGRAMME.

Let each day determine itself. There is no irritation like that of being compelled to walk to an exact time-table. Set out every morning from your inn with any determination you please—having paid your bill, and eaten heartily—but turn aside anywhere, and at any moment, to see some great sight, or to tickle the lusty trout ; sit down when you will ; retrace your steps, even, if you wish to see the great sight again ; explore the byways at all costs ; and you will have some hope of happiness. But hurry not for the mere sake of getting there.

In the folly of youth I once walked thirty-six miles in one day, and limped other twenty the next. But be

N

not deceived, no man can see the world properly who is either in a hurry or in pain. Therefore, have no programme, no time-table, and no anxiety about the mileage.

The Fourth Commandment is—WITH ALL THY WALKING THOU SHALT GET KNOWLEDGE.

Knowledge comes through the eyes, the ears, and all the senses. But many a man looks without seeing, hears without really listening, feels without being able to interpret. I have travelled in a swift car through the sublimest scenery for a whole day, looking on the most moving sights without seeing them, passing birds and beasts that I love with all my heart, but never getting a chance either to watch them or to listen to the magic of their music—a prisoner at heart all the time, to whom all natural desires are forbidden. Then I have started out to walk slowly over the same road, taking a week to cover the ground, alone, and I have gained knowledge of men and places, seen at leisure a thousand things I would otherwise have missed, and listened quietly to the music of woodland, wind, and sea. Therefore, with all your walking see that you get some understanding of the wonders of the world through which you pass. For as the writer of *Ecclesiasticus* says : " The wisdom of a learned man cometh by opportunity of leisure, and he that hath little business shall become wise."

The Fifth Commandment is—THOU SHALT CHOOSE THY COMPANIONS OF THE ROAD WITH THE UTMOST DISCRETION.

I once spent fourteen days in a small canoe, touching my companion with every movement of the body,

knowing that each motion of arms or legs meant something vital, of pleasure or pain, in wind or wave, whether
sailing or paddling : but we were well chosen ; so the
memory of that fortnight has remained a lifelong joy.
But had there not been a perfect rapport between us
we would certainly have quarrelled, and found a watery
grave through sheer incompatibility or fed-up-ness. So
is it with walking. Refuse to walk with everybody or
anybody. Choose your companion of the road as a
wise man would choose his wife. Rather travel alone
than ill-mated. The longest road can be a perfect
idyll to a solitary rambler. But every milestone
reminds you of the next when your fellow-traveller is
a bore.

The Sixth Commandment is—THOU SHALT NOT
DESPISE THE PASSER-BY.

The road is the most democratic institution in the
world. It belongs to everybody. It belonged to the
world and his wife long before the time of Abraham,
and even he, like a true tramper, went out not knowing
whither he went. The road will belong to the public
to the end of time. The greatest honour in humanity
is to be a common wayfaring man, and no one meets
the human ordinary more frequently than the tramp.
Despise no one. Pass the time of day with all. Ask
no names and seek no introductions. Share your
matches or your bread with your fellow-vagabonds.
You will find them full of surprises, as doubtless so
will they find you. And the best safeguard against
aggression is a little touch of kindness. One half of
the world does not know how the other half lives.
That is the tragedy. But this is the glory of the road—
that it belongs to all, it introduces us to all sorts and

conditions of men, and levels all ranks by the sheer necessity of circumstances. It bestows its blessings of wind and weather, beauty and companionship, on the good and the evil alike. Therefore, despise no one.

The Seventh Commandment is—THOU SHALT NOT DESTROY ANYTHING THAT IS THY NEIGHBOUR'S.

Wild flowers by the hedgerows ; song birds in the woods ; fish in the most tempting pools ; heather on the hills ; standing grain with the wind-waves rustling through it in the autumn sunshine—these are God's gifts to the wayfaring man. Enjoy them all, but destroy none. Neither shall you light fires against tree trunks, or leave them smouldering when you depart. A careless match has often set a hill-side ablaze, and an empty bottle left among the bent grass or the heather will focus the sun like a burning-glass, and so fire a whole plantation. Every time you do some damage on the road you dishonour your comrades. Therefore, leave no litter. Cover up your tracks. But, above all, destroy not anything that is your neighbour's.

The Eighth Commandment is—THOU SHALT OFTEN KEEP SILENCE IF THOU WOULDEST HEAR WHAT THE VOICE OF NATURE HAS TO SAY.

Until you can pass through the world quietly, you will never learn anything. The democracy of this new age has obtained a wondrous freedom. But when man in his first state of ignorance is let loose in the natural world he straightway celebrates his freedom with a yell. I remember walking in Switzerland long ago with a little Scots philosopher who has since then been chastened in soul by being made a professor. The tourists kept chattering like starlings about the most trivial affairs amid the most sublime scenes, until we betook ourselves to the stillness of the glaciers and the eternal snows.

You will lose all the blessings of the road if you have not the gift of silence. To pass through a wood without snapping a twig. To sit quite still at the foot of a pine tree and let a squirrel come down the trunk and look right into your eyes, wondering if you are a branch. To listen at hot noontide to the breathing of Nature as she swoons in her summer sleep. To watch the coming of the dawn from a motionless boat in a Highland loch as the light comes sweeping up behind the eastern hills and the new day is ushered in with a sigh of winds and the twittering of awaking birds. All this is only possible to a man of silence. Therefore, be still and thou shalt know.

The Ninth Commandment is—THOU SHALT BLAZE THY TRAIL WITH GOOD DEEDS.

Some one is sure to ask if you have passed this way. If so, may the question bring a word of good commendation from every cottage door, and a smile to the faces of the children in every village. Let every tramper behave so on the road that he will receive a welcome when he passes that way again. I have known a wandering man to leave the trail of the serpent behind him in Highland glens and on Hebrid Isles. Not for him the welcome back. So if you would travel the old roads again see that you walk worthily. Here is a legend for all true trampers : " I shall pass through this world but once : any good, therefore, I can do or any kindness that I can show, to any human being, let me do it now, let me not defer it, or neglect it, for I shall not pass this way again."

The Tenth Commandment is—Secure good lodgment for the night, and thy sleep shall be sweet.

The end of the longest road comes at last. With weariness, but without fatigue, the wandering man arrives at the wayside inn, hungry with health, and ready to rest. How delicious it is to " change the feet," as we say, and enjoy the evening meal, when the sun goes down behind the hills or over the tranquil sea. The last whaup is crying on the moor before it departs, and the white birds are wailing on the edge of the tide. A whiff of peat reek scents the evening air. Then, the stillness of the summer night, clean sheets, and a sound, dreamless sleep. These are the joys of the road which gold can never buy, but which are open to every wayfaring man who keeps the commandments.

SCOTTISH PILGRIMAGE IN THE LAND OF LOST CONTENT

By Rev. Dr T. RATCLIFFE BARNETT

CONTENTS

The Friendly Road. Some Vagabonds and an Angel
The Broken Butterfly. Chopin in Scotland
A Tea-cup and a Rocking-horse. Boyhood of Sir Walter Scot
The Colour of April. In Perthshire
Innerpeffray. The Story of an Ancient Library
Legends of the West Highlands. In the Sound of Mu
The Road to Argyll. Land of the Gael
Glimpses of Galloway. A Land of Colour
Loch Trool. Hills and Hillmen
Two Tragic Tales. Bladnoch and Baldoon
The Hidden Sanctuary. With the Ever-open Door
Culross. The Story of an Old Scots Burgh
Harvest of a Quiet Eye. The Beauty of Common Things
Penkill Castle. Story of a Fresco
"Hidie Holes." Of Priests, Presbyters, and Jacobites
The Last Voyage. Christmas at Sea
Dark Darmead. A Covenanting Wilderness
The Cross of Dalgarnoc. The Nithsdale Martyrs
The Monarch of the Glen. Red Deer at Home
The Black Isle. Cromarty and the Firths
By Pentland Seas. Sutherland and Caithness Coasts
Home of My Heart. Lammermuir Memories
Brave Borderland. Tragedy of Flodden
Happy Valley. The Place Where I was Born
Lismore. Home of St Moluag
A Campbell Laird. Black Duncan of the Seven Castles

With 24 full-page illustrations from photographs by Robert M. Adam.
Crown 8vo. Cloth. Pp. xiv + 208 Published price 6/- net

Press Reviews

Alike in the topographical and biographical senses his new book has a wide range. . . . Dr Barnett's deep interest in the antiquities of the regions of which he writes carries with it no hint of dull pedantry, for his motive is his preoccupation with the human background. This admirably written and well-illustrated book takes a worthy place beside *Border Byways* and *The Land of Lorne.—The Scotsman.*

Up and down the country Dr Barnett rambles—Galloway, the Lammermoors, Cromarty, Lismore are but a few of the places—talking of these and similar matters ; and his twenty-six short sketches are shot through with nostalgia of quite agreeable variety. They reflect the author's affectionate longing for times gone by, and they will stir the work-bound reader to an equally ardent longing to be walking once more in Scotland. The book contains several attractive and interesting photographs.—*Times Literary Supplement.*

Our traveller writes lucidly and uncloggedly, and with abundant historical anecdotes, about the Highlands and the Lowlands, about birds and burns and old books, about Galloway and the Covenanters, and Cromarty and Innerpeffray and the Borderland. . . . But the reader must appreciate Dr Barnett's prevailing clean, clear prose nevertheless. His style is as refreshing as a day among the heather.—*John o' London's Weekly.*

BORDER BY-WAYS
& LOTHIAN LORE

By Rev. Dr T. RATCLIFFE BARNETT

CONTENTS

RIVERS OF ROMANCE
THE HOMELY VALE
DIARY OF A TWEEDSIDE LAIRD
GANGREL'S GLORY
LONELY LOITERING
LAND OF MERLIN
HOUSE OF QUIET
FOUR ABBEYS OF THE SAIR SANCT
WINTER BEAUTY
HERMITAGE CASTLE
IN THE LAP OF THE LOWTHERS
EAST LOTHIAN
ST TRIDUANA
THE RETREAT
PENTLAND HAUNTS OF ROBERT LOUIS STEVENSON
ROARING SHEPHERD AND HIS DOG
MY WINTER SANCTUARY
WINTER WANDERINGS IN WEST LOTHIAN
CASTLE EERIE
INCHCOLM
CASTLE DUNGEONS
CRAMOND AND BARNBOUGLE
GLOSSARY

With 29 full-page illustrations from photographs by Robert M. Adam.
Crown 8vo, cloth.   Pp. xii + 228.   Published price 6/- net.

Press Reviews

Border By-ways and Lothian Lore links up past and present so pleasantly that it is indispensable to the rambler and a veritable source of refreshment to the stay-at-home, for Dr Barnett has not only the observant eye and an intimate knowledge of historical lore, but he has the art of conveying something of the speech and manners of the people and of the atmosphere of romance that hangs over all. . . . Dr Barnett is a genuine lover of nature, steeped in poetry and a fine appreciation of beauty, and his book clearly reveals it.   The illustrations, admirably reproduced from photographs by Mr Robert M. Adam, are in keeping with the lofty standard of the subject-matter.—*Weekly Scotsman.*